DATE DUE

DEMCO 38-296

THE HELL

The Life and Writings of Jane Wood Reno

WITH POLITICS

R

THE HELL ▼
The Life and Writings of Jane Wood Reno
▲ WITH POLITICS

Jane Wood Reno

Edited by George Hurchalla

PEACHTREE
PUBLISHERS

ATLANTA

Published by
PEACHTREE PUBLISHERS, LTD.
494 Armour Circle, NE
Atlanta, Georgia 30324

Cover and interior design by
Regina Dalton-Fischel

10 9 8 7 6 5 4 3 2 1

Manufactured in the United States of America

Library of Congress Cataloging-in-Publication Data
Reno, Jane Wood.
        The hell with politics : the life and writings of
Jane Wood Reno /
    Jane Wood Reno ; edited by George Hurchalla.
            p.   cm.
        ISBN 1-56145-092-8
        1. Reno, Jane Wood. 2. Women journalists—
Florida—Miami-
    -Biography.   I. Hurchalla, George.   II. Title.
    PN4874.R43A3 1994
    070′ .92—dc20
    [B]   94-3397
                                            CIP

CONTENTS

Words Spoken At The Memorial Service For Jane Wood Reno

Jane Wood Reno was no saint. One comfort that I have this afternoon is that she will not insult or emba... anyone.

She was ... the mo... momen... as I lo... the y... her ... ness ... pun... and... wo...

we came to know our friends, the Seminoles, and the magnificence and the mystery of the Everglades.

Later, I was at ... ll when she wrote ... he had

ended th... mile west at the edg... the Everglades. A mud-covered, rough-looking man walked into the yard. He had a funny way of talking and I was afriad of him, but Mother started talking with him and was imme-diately fascinated by him. He was Sippi Morris and through him

the Coun... Department, was respon-sible for the develop-mentally disabled and other fragile indigents who could not care for themselves. Mother saw the wonder and great-ness in people in this world.

Words Spoken At The ▼
Memorial Service For
▲
Jane Wood Reno

By Her Daughter Janet Reno
December 23, 1992

Wynken, Blynken, and Nod one night
Sailed off in a wooden shoe.—
Sailed on a river of crystal light
Into a sea of dew.
"Where are you going, and what do you wish?"
The Old Man asked the three.
"We have come to fish for the herring fish
That live in this beautiful sea;
Nets of silver and gold have we!"
Said Wynken,
Blynken,
And Nod.

She was not an elegant woman in the usual sense, but she had a rare sense of strong beauty and how to create it. The house she built with her own hands still stands and the beautiful cypress paneling is as warm and glowing as the day she built it. She could see beauty when obscured and she took an old worm-eaten piece of driftwood mahogany and fashioned it into the most beautiful mantelpiece which still presides over her kitchen. And that house was strong. On the morning of August 24, 1992, at about 6:30, I turned to her and said, "Old Woman, you built one hell of a house." It came through Andrew losing only one shingle and some screens.

▲ Photo on previous spread: Jane Wood Reno and eldest daughter Janet in the mid 1980s, in front of the house Jane built by hand, working from 1949 to 1951. This house later withstood hurricane Andrew, one of the century's most devastating storms, with losses totaling only one shingle and a few window screens.

I can see her so clearly sitting beside my bed when I was a little girl at 111 South Eleventh Street just a few blocks from here, soothing me to sleep with these words. And for the rest of her life she took us to fish for the herring fish. Her nets of silver and gold were a battered aqualung, a brown and white, blue-eyed pony who pulled a buggy at a trot, cars that broke down and which she regularly got stuck in the mud because that lady got herself stuck in the mud more than anyone I know, sailboats that she caulked herself and trains and planes.

And she took us to "Spanish waters, Spanish waters, you are ringing in my ears like the slow sweet piece of music of grey forgotten years..." She took us "Across the seas to Wonderland." She took us over the purple moor and to the Old Inn yard and whenever I see the moon as a ghostly galleon I will think of the Highwayman, Bess and Mother.

She took us to Alph the Sacred River which "ran through caverns mea-sureless to man down to a sunless sea." To get there, she took us down the dirt roads of North Florida around the last bend to find a blue spring of which she wrote:

> Funnel shaped, they shade from crystal water on the sandy shore, to sky blue, then to the deepest royal blue at the center.... You can float over the shafts where the cool water wells and see specks of mica glinting on sandy floors of caves, 40, 60, 90 feet below, as though you looked through air. You can see the expression in the eyes of the bream, the curl in whiskers of the catfish, count mullet scales. The water from the spring streams away through the woods to the nearby river....

> You may make no poetry, catch no fish, but... a time of playing hooky by the springs of the Suwanee River country will be a blue jewel in your memory for as long as you remember beauty.

She loved us all so much, her children, her family and her friends. She could say "I love you" better than anyone I know. Even in the last days as we came on to her porch she would say "Hello, my Darling. I love you!"

But she was stern. An aunt once asked us why we children were so good (which is debatable). My brother Bobby replied, "Why, Aunt Adelle, our Mother beat us with a bridle." And so she did.

Jane Wood Reno was no saint. One comfort that I have this afternoon is that she will not insult or embarrass anyone. She was responsible for the most excruciating moments of my life. But as I look back over all the years almost all of her outrageous foolishness was directed at puncturing the pomp and arrogance of this world.

She could pick out the wonderful people of this world. One afternoon when I was little we were sitting out in the front yard on Kendall Drive which ended then just a half mile west at the edge of the Everglades. A mud-covered, rough-looking man walked into the yard. He had a funny way of talking and I was afraid of him, but Mother started talking with him and was immediately fascinated by him. He was Sippi Morris and through him we came to know our friends, the Seminoles, and the magnificence and the mystery of the Everglades.

Later, I was at Cornell when she wrote to tell me that she had met a lady I must work for in the coming summer because she was such a wonderful person. I came home after the first day of work and said the lady wasn't so special—she seemed thin lipped, cold and remote. But the next day I discovered how wonderful she was. She was Corinne Gautier Davis, one of the great saints of the world who, as Director of the Placement Division of the County Welfare Department, was responsible for the developmentally disabled and other fragile indigents who could not care for themselves. Mother saw the wonder and greatness in people in this world.

She was fearless and unafraid of anything. After she walked 104 miles up the Florida shore, she wrote:

> So… it might be that some day I shall be drowned by the sea, or die of pneumonia from sleeping out at night, or be robbed and strangled by strangers. These things happen. Even so, I shall be ahead because of trusting the beach, the night, and strangers.

She led her children on, never holding us back for fear. Shortly after Jacques Cousteau invented the aqualung, Mother decided we should learn how to use it. In the process she covered a story of Hope Root who dived one day to try to set a world record. And she wrote:

> Hope Root dived into the most beautiful world he knew and died in the royal blue Gulf Stream yesterday.

> Do you think he was crazy to literally find a heaven down under the water? You ought to go and look. There isn't anything ugly down there.

Everything's quiet, every movement is smooth, every color is quite perfect. On down there is just one color, the perfect blue of evening.

You can go down into that world and live for a while in your eyes, be
completely satisfied just to look. You are cradled, weightless, down there
in the home all life on this earth came from.

Even after watching him dive and die she took us down to Hens and
Chickens, to the beautiful coral heads and the concrete barge. When Maggy
dived under the barge so Mother couldn't see her bubbles, she did not panic
and tell us to stop. She has let us go on to see the world.

She was not an elegant woman in the usual sense, but she had a rare sense
of strong beauty and how to create it. The house she built with her own hands
still stands and the beautiful cypress paneling is as warm and glowing as the
day she built it. She could see beauty when obscured and she took an old
worm-eaten piece of driftwood mahogany and fashioned it into the most beautiful mantelpiece which still presides over her kitchen. And that house was
strong. On the morning of August 24, 1992, at about 6:30, I turned to her and
said, "Old Woman, you built one hell of a house." It came through Andrew
losing only one shingle and some screens.

She had such insight into the human soul. I went to live in Germany for
a year when I was thirteen. Before I left she told me about homesickness and
what I should expect and how my heart would feel wrenched. It hurt to be
homesick and I don't know how I could have stood it had she not told me
what to expect.

If she loved her children, she worshipped her grandchildren, and it was
wonderful to see her hold her great-granddaughter, her blessed Kymberly. She
said the reason you had children was so that you could have grandchildren and
spoil them rotten and feed them ice cream for breakfast. She took them across
the world and she loved them dearly.

She knew she was dying although she would forget the fact when conve-
nient. She did not fear death. But she loved life to the end. Even in these past
weeks as I walked with her across her porch, she looked out across the yard,
feeling the warm sun and seeing the sparkling blue of the sky against the tapes-
try of green, and she would say, "I love this world."

She was life itself to me. Whenever I asked myself what life was for or what
the meaning of life was, I needed only look over at her, or call her if I was away
from her, or in the last days reach over and hold her old and gnarled hand, to
know the answer. Hello my Darling. We love you very much.

▲ PREFACE ▼

There are some wonderful things that have happened to me in my life, things that I could never have made up. And many delightful people have told me things they said happened, things that I don't think they made up.

Almost anybody who has been a reporter, a social worker, a press agent, a Cub Scout den mother, and a mother of a number of children has had such things happen, been told such stories. All tugboatmen I ever met have a fund.

And I will be delighted to live as long as I can find people to tell me stories that have inherent in them this wonderfulness that doesn't depend on the way they are told.

I love well-invented stories. Wonderfully told tales that could never have happened, spun out of the insides of a creator, do delight me. And before everything else I revere poems, which you do not pick up over drinks, stories, or talking to tugboatmen. But I cannot invent or create stories, or write enough poems to please me. (I only ever wrote two I liked, and lost one.)

It has seemed to me, however, that in both gratitude and pleasure, I might write some of the stories that have happened and have so delighted me. What I have wanted to save are the accounts that remind me of the driftwood we collected so avidly one summer we spent at Traver's place on the Keys. There was nothing I could do to or with those silvery, sand-etched and sunbleached boards and logs that could have made them any prettier or more satisfying.

Sippi walked around this gator hole and grabbed a
four-foot gator by the tail. It was that easy. "Just keep
pulling on his tail so he can't reverse ends on you and
you're all right," he explained. "With a big one," he
said, "you j... him, grab him by what would be his
neck if he ... and roll with him."

Sippi s...
of the he...
provoke...
lies in ...
shakes...

lizard...
him...
paw...
hi...
h...

gator-gr...
ed now, and it's a...
like to see alligators in the...
mal. Gators make gator holes and...
out. They'll keep water in a gator hole, and...
drink not only for other wild animals but for cattle in...
lot of that country out there." He waved west and north
of Miami. "In a drought a gator hole means money to a
cattleman."

How to Install
a Glass Eye in an
Angry Crocodile

▼

▲

Between Land, Sea, and

What is it like to live halfway between sea and sky, in a tower far from land?

To Carysfort Reef lighthouse we took that question. Six miles off the northern end of Key Largo, it is one of the chain of seven notable structures along the Florida reefs that warn the big steamers away from the shallow ledge that once made the wreckers' cry familiar to the Keys.

The light is supported by four immense iron pilings. Its range is sixteen miles. A little less than halfway up the

tow
ing
cre
the
gas o
refrig
and s
ley is
room
gasolir
big bat
turn ke

Abo
deck, i
phones,
library, a
house ke
Also on t

ŞURE THING

One afternoon when I was on
y side at the *News*, the phone
ιg, and a fellow said, "Is this Jane
ood? I'd like to talk to you. I have
ιething I think will interest you
y much."

So I told him that I'd be there
t thirty minutes and that I'd
for him.

ιd after about that interval, this
man came in, headed purpose-
for my desk, sat down, and
luced himself. He had the
most honest, trusting blue
ιd a voice you had to believe.
e only other time I ever had
ones was in Hope Root, who
ιt day. They said, in effect,

"Everything is now. There had
never been anything more important than today. This is the whole
truth I tell you."

He looked at me with a glance
that opened his heart and spirit and
said, "Do I look crazy to you?"

And I answered as straightforwardly as he, "No, certainly not!"

He said, "I ask that because I
have something to tell you that you
may not believe. I have discovered
how to predict the future."

He sat back quietly. I sighed and
said, "How about let's going downstairs and getting a cup of coffee?"

We got coffee and sat down in the
cafeteria. He said it was like this:

▲ Photo on previous spread: The world's first underwater interview. Jane Wood
Reno uses a slate and a slate pencil to interview Ed Fisher during his twenty-four-
hour dive.

SIPPI

**HE'S GOT AN ANSWER TO ABOUT EVERY EMERGENCY
THAT MEETS A MAN ROAMING THE FLORIDA WILDS**

I. How To Install A Glass Eye in an Angry
Crocodile.

II. Detailed Instructions on Grunting Up and then Relaxing
Alligators.

III. About the Circumstances Surrounding the Invention of
the Sippi Super Suction Snakebite System.

If Sippi Morris writes his memoirs, these well could be chapter headings. But
since Sippi will probably spend all his spare time for the rest of his life in the
Everglades and adjacent wildernesses, posterity may never hear from him—
and so, it may be a better idea to set down some of his experiences here.

In working hours Sippi Morris is M. M. Morris, territory manager for a
national tire and rubber company, and he lives in the genteel suburban surroundings of Coral Gables. But he is one of that tribe of men from all walks of
life who are possessed by a passion for woods and swamps and the special skies
that arch over all that which is wild.

In his all-but-sea-going jeep, he has poked his nose into the parts of
Florida that see far more Indians than white men. The equipment of this jeep
is a marvel: the most oversized tires; a winch on the front bumper driven by

an electric generator, with a long steel cable to wind himself out of holes; special inventions of his own on the motor that make him able to drive through three feet of water; a house for his dogs; a device that works off the exhaust and makes and keeps hot eighteen cups of coffee at a time, as well as keeping his sandwiches hot, too; and last but not least, two iceboxes.

Sippi not only invented a lot of his swamp buggy, he helped invent the annual Naples Swamp Buggy Race.

The uninitiated who do not savor the pleasure of getting well-covered with mud and mosquitoes sometimes confuse swamp buggies with air boats, if they have never seen either. But air boats are actually flat-bottomed little skiffs, powered by an airplane motor and propeller. They are made to skim over the water and wet grass of the saw-grass Everglades. The buggies are designed to roll through mud.

The race is part of three days of parades and activities. It is run on a gray marl track that turns into a glue-like soup after the first buggies run on it.

Judges on horseback will patrol the course, and the rules and regulations of the race say that their duty is to see that "there is no unnecessary foul play on the part of the drivers." Necessary foul play is apparently allowed since there is considerable informal betting on the races, both in confederate money from cereal boxes, and in green money from the U.S. Treasury. There are always hot arguments.

Sippi can argue if necessary. He once convinced a murderer in the Dade County jail to give him his breakfast. That's another story. He ended up in jail because he was hunting with Dade County Sheriff Jimmy Sullivan. The sheriff couldn't go to jail and someone had to, so Sippi volunteered. He was covered with deer blood and he told the murderer, "They say I killed three, but I only killed one."

Heavy-set, light-footed, Sippi is a man who can slough through mud and saw grass all day and then sit by a campfire over coffee and spin stories of strange and funny happenings in the wilds. For thirty years, since he came to this state, he has been exploring Florida wild lands, so he doesn't have to throw myth or hearsay into his accounts—he hews right straight down along the line of truth.

Sippi has hunted everything from wild pig to panther. He's hatched alligator eggs in a downtown apartment. He was lost in the Everglades for three days and nights, and slept down in the water because of the mosquitoes, with his head on a log. He speaks a little Seminole and has been to the green corn dance.

Recently Sippi consented to give us a lesson on Alligator handling. We went out to a gator hole, not twenty minutes drive from the court house, and he showed how to grunt them up.

"Now, the Indians do it better than I can, they grunt deep in their chest," he explained. "But here's the way I do it."

Sippi made a loud smacking noise with his lips against his forearm.

"The way I figure it is this. You don't have to sound like a gator, you just have to make a curious noise for him to come out and see what's it all about. A gator has a brain about the size of a marble—got more gray matter in his backbone than in his head—but he's awful curious."

Sippi walked around this gator hole and grabbed a four-foot gator by the tail. It was that easy. "Just keep pulling on his tail so he can't reverse ends on you and you're all right," he explained. "With a big one," he said, "you jump him, grab him by what would be his neck if he had any neck, and roll with him."

Sippi squatted down and took hold of the gator back of the head. His hand inched forward until it held the provoked little saurian's jaws closed. "Their strength lies in closing their jaws, not in opening them. If he shakes his head, shake your hand with him."

Then Sippi proceeded to turn the primour-plated lizard over and held him firmly on his back, just held him there. Within fifty seconds you could see the gator's paws go limp, see his whole body relax. Then Sippi took his hand away, and the gator just lay there as though hypnotized.

"Why, it's magic!" we shouted. "Why does he relax?"

"Just gives up. Got no sense," Sippi explained.

"Many's the time I've caught and skinned, but not anymore," he went on, when we'd settled down after the gator-grunting lesson. "They are pretty rigidly protected now, and it's a good thing. It's not only that people like to see alligators in the wilds. They are a useful animal. Gators make gator holes and keep them cleaned out. They'll keep water in a gator hole, and that means drink not only for other wild animals but for cattle in a lot of that country out there." He waved west and north of Miami. "In a drought a gator hole means money to a cattleman."

We prompted him about gator catching.

"Well, the worst time I ever had was with a crocodile, not with a gator. I went down to an aquarium, way back yonder in the twenties, when the American Legion was coming to town. And I said, "Captain, you don't have a crocodile to show the Legionaires. Ought to have a crocodile."

5
▲

"Where'll I get one?" said the captain.

"I'll catch you one for sixty-five dollars," I said, and I went out and shot a nine-foot crocodile, meant to crease his skull and shot him in the eye. We tied his jaws together with some sash cord and took him down to the aquarium. A crocodile's meaner than a gator, and getting him out of the car, he gave my leg a whack with the side of his jaw that laid it open."

Sippi paused while we examined a twenty-year-old-looking scar on his ankle.

"I can't use a one-eyed crocodile," the captain says.

"Captain," I told him, "I'll get you the mate to this one."

"So," continued Sippi, "I conferred with a taxidermist and ordered me some glass crocodile eyes from a taxidermist supply house in New Jersey. In the meantime, I put the crocodile in a cage in my back yard. I put a little old white rooster in there for him to eat, and he wouldn't even touch him. The rooster roosted on the crocodile's tail every night. I had to ram meat down his throat with a broomstick to keep him alive.

"Finally, the eyes came, and I get in there in the cage, and rassle one into this fellow's socket. It wasn't quite big enough, though, and it rolled around, so that the slit in one of his eyes was vertical, and one horizontal. Not so good. Finally I get a bigger one in, and it looked pretty good, so I took him down to the aquarium, and quick-like dumped him in the tank before the captain could look at him good. The crocodile, of course, swam around so that he could look at the captain through the glass side of the tank out of his good eye, and nobody ever did get a real good look at him head-on, so they could compare eyes."

From here we went into the chronicle of the invention of the Sippi Super-Suction Snakebite System. Some years ago, Sippi was hunting birds in the Devil's Garden country, east of Ft. Myers, on horseback. When he dismounted to make a shot over his dog, the rattlesnake bit him, two inches above the knee. He grabbed the dog with one hand, and shot the snake with the other.

"There I had on a fifty-six dollar pair of boots, and above them, a pair of snakebite leggins, and I got bit." He showed us the white scars, two inches apart, where he had cut the fang punctures. "Since then I'd just as soon hunt in tennis shoes.

"I made my cuts too wide," he said, "and it spoiled the suction of the snakebite kit I had with me. So I tied a boot-lace above the bite, got on the horse and rode back nineteen miles to the house of the fellow I was hunting with. Fortunately, the boot-lace broke now and then, and finally I tied a bandana around my leg for a tourniquet, and it slipped now and then, or I'd probably have had gangrene.

"That's one of the great dangers of a fellow's treating his snakebite. If he leaves the tourniquet on too long, there's far more danger from gangrene from the blood being cut off than there is that he'll die from the snakebite. Ought to loose the tie for a minute or so every fifteen minutes.

"Anyhow, we got back to the house of the fellow I was hunting with, and he offered me a drink—he was a moonshiner.

"Instead I took a funnel and piece of rubber tubing from his equipment. I went out to my car, hooked the rubber tubing on to my windshield wiper, put the funnel over both fang marks, and let the thing suck on my leg for about an hour.

"Then I went to the Ft. Myers hospital and asked them to give me a tetanus shot and they could hardly believe I'd been bit, my system showed so little signs of rattlesnake poisoning."

As a result of this brilliant inspiration with the windshield wiper, Sippi invented and sporadically manufactures the Sippi Super-Suction Snakebite System. Compact in a small leather box, it consists of two little glass cups, connected by rubber tubing and a glass Y-tube with a venom trap attached to a joint which may be plugged in immediately to the connection to an automobile windshield wiper. The car is started, the wiper turned on, and the suction is strong and continuous enough to draw flesh a half inch up into the glass cups. A stiff rubber bulb comes with the kit for use with the outfit before you can reach your car.

"Besides the windshield wiper idea, the two advantages of my kit are the venom trap, and the fact that with the two cups you can apply suction at the points at which both fangs enter. No working on one puncture while the poison gets into you from the other," Sippi explained.

"If you can't stand to cut yourself, there's enough suction here to drag out most of the venom, but it's better to make a couple of little cuts at the points where the fangs go in, quarter inch deep and about a quarter inch wide—and be careful not to cut any veins or arteries."

We looked the whole invention over, and watched the way it works, and our respect for the human race went up. Any race that can produce a Sippi Morris is something—really special.

Since then Sippi has invented the piddle-pack.

But above all, Sippi is swamp buggies.

If you sawed off the top of his head and lifted it up, and looked down

7
▲

inside—you wouldn't see brains like most men have. You would see four or five little swamp buggies running round and round inside his head. And you had better put the top back on quick, or he would be asking you to help him put chains on the buggies.

And the lure of the buggies is the lure of the saw-grass Everglades and the game-filled land of the Cypress Swamps.

For Sippi, the rare breed of swamp lovers, are the lines of Hopkins.

> *What would the world be, once bereft*
> *Of wet and of wilderness? Let them be left.*
> *O let them be left, wilderness and wet;*
> *Long live the weed and the wilderness wet.*

MEN

To start their new year right, eleven men went into the Florida wilderness with knife and axe, flint and steel, to live off the land. They took no food of commerce, carried no shelter or blankets.

Ten of them were very young men, with an average age of thirteen years. The wilderness they survived in is the prettiest in south Florida—along Fisheating Creek where it runs from Palmdale east into Lake Okeechobee. They walked out grinning after their four days of survival camp, and reported, as they plied themselves with double-rich malted milk shakes— "Too easy."

This was the fabled, annual, live-off-the-land survival trip of Boy Scout Troop 69 of Princeton. Some of the young campers were trained veterans, some were tenderfeet.

The veterans have trained by being lost in the Everglades, being lost in the great Smoky Mountains, and not being lost in thirty-five feet of water at Hen and Chickens rocks of Matecumbe Key. They have trained by avoiding huge falling pine trees they chopped to build their own cabin in the woods near Goulds. They have trained by eating their own cooking at each weekly scout meeting.

Scoutmaster Norman Benson trained for the role by being born one of nine brothers. He runs an electrician's shop at Perrine in his spare time. Assistant scoutmaster Fred Mowry lives with a pet owl on his front porch, tolerated by his mother. Nineteen-year-old Mowry has the reputation of being able to con a coon down a tree into his hands with soft talk. The rest of the survivors were Terry Hinkle, Tom Frasier, Jack Bible, Jerry Kramer, Alfred

Kramer, Gerald Eicher, Mark Reno and Herbert Landrum.

They lived out a dream that millions of men have lived with since they left caves—the dream of being self-sufficient.

Maybe you want to try this for the good of your spirit, or your waistline. Saints have chosen the wilderness, and survival camping is a guaranteed fat remover, ascetic or not. Maybe the bomb will fall someday that will drive us all to living off the land.

So the experience of Troop 69 can be useful to you.

First come committees, naturally. The shelter committee took care of hut building, digging the water hole, firewood, latrine and fire building. The animal fowl committee took care of snares and baits for coons, pigs, rabbits, and birds. The vegetable committee took care of coontie root preparation, palmetto salad, cattail roots, wild citrus and cypress tea. The fish committee made fish lines, hooks and fish traps.

Here is how the committees' work turned out in practice.

SHELTER: A peaked hut thatched with palmettos keeps the drizzle off. They were glad it wasn't tested by a hard rain. Lack of nails was the challenge. They thoroughly braced two forked poles to support the ridge pole, and tied the ridge pole in the forks. Rafters were long thin saplings laid from ground to ridge pole tied together at the top. Thinner saplings were tied close together across the rafters as purlins. The palmetto "shingles" were cut with their yard-long stems left on. The stems were woven twice through the sapling purlins, and they stayed on.

FOOD: One of the staples of the diet was baked coontie flour. They made it beforehand from the roots of the wild coontie plant that looks like a little sage palm. The root of the plant is as big as a potato and poisonous raw. They peeled these roots, shredded them fine, soaked them for a half hour to an hour, and poured off the pink water. After four or five soakings, when the water was no longer pink but milky, they poured the last soaking through a cloth.

After this straining they let the milky water settle an hour. A fine white flour settled out. They poured off the liquid, dried the flour, and packed it in bamboo canteens. They baked it for bread. They blamed the cook because, though it was edible, it was not tasty.

Cattail roots, cabbage palm hearts and sweet and sour oranges from an ancient grove gone wild were tasty and were the staples of their diet. They got protein from eating little minnows whole. These canapes were not on the program. Report says: "Minnows tickled all the way down."

They caught a very small suckling pig, and were chased by an angry sow.

They had to climb trees fast, piglet under arm, and outwait their prey's mother. After they studied the piglet, they decided he was too little to go around, too young to die. They reported he was red haired, like Tommy Frasier, and cute, and they let him go.

INCONVENIENCES: Due to chiggers, and homesick discussion by tenderfeet of favorite foods, they did not sleep well. They took naps during the day in the sun, windscreened by the palmettos. Once they woke up to find a flock of buzzards sitting over them.

"The buzzards were just waiting for us to die, but once we woke up to find a big old boar hog with tusks about three inches long about to eat Kramer."

Homesickness is routine among the tenderfeet on these trips, explain the veterans. Its symptoms: tears for no good reason. First aid for this ill: a few good-natured jeers without edge or barb.

They saw a bobcat. No danger. They saw four magnificent sandhill cranes as big as baby ostriches. No danger. They caught a big indigo snake. No danger. But he got out of the sack before they could eat him. From previous experience they report that well-cooked snake is like fried frog legs.

One boy got a little sick from eating gallberries.

A poll of parents of these survivors produced one chief point of agreement about their physical condition on their return. If they were thinner in the waist, their chests were so swollen with pride that they actually seemed bigger.

Sure Thing

One afternoon when I was on city side at the *News*, the phone rang, and a fellow said, "Is this Jane Wood? I'd like to talk to you. I have something I think will interest you very much."

So I told him that I'd be there about thirty minutes and that I'd wait for him.

And after about that interval, this nice man came in, headed purposefully for my desk, sat down, and introduced himself. He had the nicest, most honest, trusting blue eyes, and a voice you had to believe.

The only other time I ever had those tones was in Hope Root, who died that day. They said, in effect, "Everything is now. There had never been anything more important than today. This is the whole truth I tell you."

He looked at me with a glance that opened his heart and spirit and said, "Do I look crazy to you?"

And I answered as straightforwardly as he, "No, certainly not!"

He said, "I ask that because I have something to tell you that you may not believe. I have discovered how to predict the future."

He sat back quietly. I sighed and said, "How about let's going downstairs and getting a cup of coffee?"

We got coffee and sat down in the cafeteria. He said it was like this:

"I'm a watchmaker from Lexington, Kentucky. My family is very religious, and I am very religious. I have been studying the Bible, and that is where I found how to predict the future. You have to believe the Bible, don't you?"

"It begins like this," he said, "and you have to believe this," and he wrote on a paper napkin, "Man plus woman equals God."

"You have to believe that," he said, and I nodded.

"So I don't make much money, and we are buying a house, and my little girl loves the school she's in. But if we lose the house, we'll have to get an apartment, and she'll be in another school. So what can you do if you can predict the future?"

"The stock market?" I ventured.

"No, the horse races," he said. "You understand, we are very religious people. My family would be shocked by gambling. But I would never gamble. I know. This is not gambling. But I borrowed $1,200 from my brother-in-law to come here. They don't know. They would be shocked. But it's not gambling."

My Miami morality raised its funny twisted head and said to me alone, "But this isn't right, betting on a sure thing," but I stayed quiet.

He plunged ahead, with this arterial spurt, this total confiding, "I don't make it fast enough. I'll lose the house if I don't have the money in three days. And it takes me so long to work out the daily double. It's mathematical. I've stayed up all night the last three nights working it out. I've won. But it takes so long, with what I have. I don't have the time. I'll lose the house. My little girl will have to go to another school."

My mouth was getting dry. "Why do you come to me?" I said like somebody in a book.

"I asked the telephone operator if anybody on the *Miami News* had won the Big Story award, and she said, 'Yes, Milt Sosin and Jane Wood.' And I asked for him and he wasn't in, and then I asked for you. Because I knew whoever won the Big Story award is a good reporter and could help me."

Milt and I are good reporters, but my mouth was getting dryer.

"What do you want me to do?" I said.

"You must know somebody who has a lot of money who would be glad to know how to predict the future," he said. "I want you to get somebody like that to give me the money to bet, and I will split fifty-fifty. It takes so much time, and I haven't much time. And I haven't had any sleep for two nights, and I've got this money I won, but it's not enough. So maybe the newspaper would put up the money because this is a wonderful thing."

He started writing more formulas on the paper napkin, and I have a sneaking notion that if I could remember where he was headed I could buy a new car and stop worrying about college tuitions.

"Or," he said, "you must know somebody with money."

"What shall I do?" he said.

"It takes eight or ten hours to work out all the formulas," he said, "and I'm so sleepy. I haven't had any sleep for two days or two nights. Should I go back to the hotel and work out tomorrow's winners now, or should I have a nap first? If I sleep long I won't have time to work them out. I could only sleep four or five hours, because I have to be out to the track for the first race. You do understand it's not gambling?"

I was right shattered. I have a daughter I adore, and I found her crying herself to sleep one time because she had to go to a school she didn't like and wanted to go so much to another one she loved, and it was because of where we lived.

And I thought that the tie that bound my watchmaker friend to the future was more delicate than a spider web. He was drugged with fatigue, living in the moment. There was the watchmaking and the religion and the predicting the future. But I had finally recognized where he got his terribly moving conviction, his trust, his belief, his sincerity. It came from lack of sleep.

At that moment, there was no future for him beyond the next day or so.

"I'm so tired," he said, "I'm afraid I'll make a mistake in the figures for the daily double tomorrow. I haven't got time to figure anything but the daily double. That takes eight or ten hours."

I got up. "Come with me," I said, in my Cub Scout den mother tone. "I'm going to take you to your hotel, and you're going to sleep. It'll be time enough, after you've had five or six hours sleep, to figure the race tomorrow and get out to the track. You have to have some sleep. You are so sleepy, you'll be slowed up in your figures. You can't figure accurately when you're tired. Just leave word with your desk clerk to wake you up about ten o'clock tonight, and you'll have plenty of time to figure, and eat breakfast, and get out to the track for the first race."

I drove east downtown to take him to his hotel, and the whole courthouse was pink. The light stone was pink, and the windows were pink. The sun was setting behind me, but it was a real rosy pink and one of the prettiest things I ever saw in Miami, in all our quick gorgeous sunsets. And it didn't make me feel a darn bit better to know there wasn't going to be a bit of pink there tomorrow morning.

I let him out, and told him with quiet authority that the thing to do was to sleep five or six hours, and to call me tomorrow. Isaac Newton, a devoutly religious man, was distressed because he was unable to figure out the nature of the force, gravity, that holds things together. My distress that evening and the next morning was similar, but not quite the same. I was not at all sure that

15
▲

there was any force, however mysterious or unknown, strong enough to hold my watchmaker friend on this earth and out of an orbit that would take him forever away, if he didn't sleep, and didn't win, and didn't get to keep that house.

So it was with great relief that I heard the lightness in his voice the next afternoon when he telephoned. "I took your advice," he said, "but the room clerk didn't call me. And I slept till eight in the morning, from 5:30 P.M. yesterday. And then I began the figuring. And I had time to work out the first half of the daily double, but not the second. So I guessed on the second, and bet it all. And I lost. The first horse came in. But not the second. So it's back to watchmaking in Lexington for me. I saved enough to get home on. But I'll think of something else."

And his voice told me he had a future, again, and he was living in it. I stopped shaking inside, for him.

Between Land, Sea, and Sky

What is it like to live halfway between sea and sky, in a tower far from land?

To Carysfort Reef lighthouse we took that question. Six miles off the northern end of Key Largo, it is one of the chain of seven notable structures along the Florida reefs that warn the big steamers away from the shallow ledge that once made the wreckers' cry familiar to the Keys.

The light is supported by four immense iron pilings. Its range is sixteen miles. A little less than halfway up the tower are the two-decked living quarters of the lighthouse crew. On the lower deck is the galley with a big bottled gas cooking range, an electric refrigerator, kitchen table, and sink. Adjoining the galley is the bathroom and the room in which two Kohler gasoline generators keep the big batteries charged that in turn keep the light burning.

Above this, on the upper deck, is the office, with phones, radios, barometer, library, and journals of lighthouse keepers long dead. Also on the upper deck are three bedrooms with two single beds in each. The roof of this deck traps enough rain to serve, stored, as drinking and washing water.

And beyond each door and window the sea stretches away, with the most varied shades of browns, greens, and blues, to meet the arch of a glorious sky.

Our hosts at Carysfort light were Walter Johnson, engineman 2nd class, and Harold Turner, fireman, members of the Coast Guard. As hosts they would make a Chinese mandarin or a Southern lady seem sullen boors.

Walter came seven miles to the dock of the Ocean Reef Club, to pick us up in the lighthouse launch. They invited us to lunch—beans, stew, coleslaw, and coffee. They refused our help with dish-washing. They showed us over their domain. We examined the light and Harold's collection of pin-up girls.

Walter pointed out faded entries in the lighthouse Bible. In brown ink and spidery, copperplate handwriting, lightkeepers had entered their names, their comings and their goings for almost a century.

And everything they did for us was filled with a very real pleasure in our company that is the essence of hospitality. No wine could be more heart-warming than their regret that we must leave.

Four Miami boys who were out on the reef spear fishing tied up to one of the pilings of the light and asked if they might haul up a two-hundred-pound Jewfish and gut him there. Harold helped the boys hook block and tackle to the fish and haul him up. Walter invited them up for beans and a Coca-Cola, too.

As we ate, they said regretfully, "Ah, if only the Chief was here. He's a wonderful cook. You ought to taste his candied sweet potatoes."

And again, "If only the Chief was here. He could tell you wonderful stories about lighthouses. He's been twenty-three years a lighthouse keeper."

Over coffee they told us about the Chief and lighthouse duty. The Chief is M.L. Bierer, chief lighthousekeeper at Carysfort. He is a civilian, and his job comes under civil service. Walter, Harold, and Don Lundstrom, seaman, are coast guardsmen assigned to the lighthouse for a nine-month tour of duty.

Each man serves a twenty-eight-day stretch at the lighthouse, and then gets nine days leave. Three men are thus always on duty.

On the day that we were there Chief Bierer was taking his stretch of freedom with his family. His wife, four children, and numerous grandchildren live in Miami.

Walter is second in command of the lighthouse crew. He has a wife, a son, and a daughter in Jacksonville. "I'm going to bring my boy down here for a visit this summer if they leave me at the light. He's twelve years old, and he'll love it."

"This is a vacation to me. I've been here since April. Maybe I shouldn't say how much I like it, or the Coast Guard will decide they need an engine man in Alaska. But I came here out of the engine room of the cutter Black Hawk. I was clammy white and didn't have any appetite from being down in the engine room all the time. We were lucky on that cutter if we got a forty-eight-hour pass every six months. We were so crowded down below that it was bed-lam, couldn't read, couldn't write letters."

Walter's eyes caressed his surroundings as he said, "But I like this. There's peace, we dress like we please, we swim, we get along with each other. I eat breakfast now. I have a huge appetite."

Walter, though he is only in his thirties, has served twelve years in the Coast Guard. In the war he was on an L.S.T. in the Pacific, from Guadalcanal to Saipan. When he last reenlisted for a three-year stretch, he was sent to Alaska for six months. "This is the best duty I've had."

Harold's objection to the lighthouse is succinct: "I'm getting lazy, it's ruining my morals. I guess I'm too young for this." He's twenty-three, his wife lives in Atlanta, and his daughter is a year old. He reenlisted in the Coast Guard in April, 1949, after a three-year stretch that ended in 1947. He hoped for an assignment as a mechanic, for he had worked at that trade at the Atlanta post office.

"Now I've dreamed up a wish that they'll transfer me to the Coast Guard band at New London, Connecticut. I play a hot trumpet." He demonstrated and he's right. He can also play the tenor sax, the alto sax, and the git fiddle, and catch fish better than anybody else in the crew.

Harold grants that a lighthouse is a fine place for practicing the saxophone, if the crew is tolerant, which this one is.

We looked at the library, two shelves of varied volumes. *The Circular Staircase* and *Moby Dick* seemed appropriate.

We picked up the latter, a worn copy and it fell open to a page that says: "But let me have one more good round look aloft here at the sea; there's time for that. An old, old sight, and yet somehow so young...The same—the same—the same to Noah as to me. There's a soft shower to leeward. Such lovely leewardings! They must lead somewhere—to something else than common land, more palmy than the palms."

We put down the book reluctantly, and, with great reluctance, left the lighthouse.

HERO

Once upon a time back in the olden days of the early 1950s, some staid airlines still had stewards. Men. One day one of the stewards discovered, just after the plane had taken off from Tampa, that the door of the plane wasn't quite closed. He pulled it to close it, and the door opened and pulled him out of the plane.

It was the kind of a door that was hinged at the bottom and opened down and out. He held on and got back safe, and I was sent to interview him.

He was dark, young, handsome, and extremely articulate.

I said, "My, you are a hero."

He said, "I am not impressed. I am the son of the Roumanian doctor who was the personal physician of Queen Marie of Roumania. I am a naturalized American citizen, and was a member of the 82nd Airborne Division when they jumped at the Battle of Bastogne. I was given a hero's welcome when my contingent arrived back in Boston. I am not impressed with being a hero."

"My goodness," I said, "How did you feel when you were hanging there?"

"I won't tell you that," he replied promptly. "I think I can sell that to one of three TV programs which I have contacted. What I won't tell you is how I felt. I don't make a lot of money, and I think I might make some money out of how I felt."

"Well, my goodness, I see what you mean, could you tell me what happened—as to the mechanics, that is."

"I was holding on to the handle of the door, and it was pulled out, and I hung to the door. We were over the bay of Tampa. The door was held in position by a chain running from the frame of the plane to the door, and it held the door at a right angle to the plane, roughly horizontal with the ground. I found myself hanging on below the door, holding to the edge of the door with my hands, and dangling down above the bay."

"For heaven's sakes," I said, "could you tell me how you got back safely?"

"Yes, I can tell you that. The only difficult part was during the period in which I was hanging there, trying to swing my leg up over the door and around that chain. That was hard. But once I did it, I knew I was okay. They tried to pull the door back in to the plane, but of course, they couldn't.

"I knew that there was only about three feet between the bottom of the door, when opened, and the ground when the plane landed, and as I hung on with most of my body beneath the door and my leg hooked around the chain, going down I was indeed apprehensive. However, the pilot set it down like a crate of eggs, very smooth, and I was perfectly okay. The man on the ground waiting with the ambulance ran out to meet me. He was much weaker than I was. He looked like he was going to faint. I did have a few moments of reaction, shock, going into town, but I was perfectly okay thereafter."

"My goodness," I said, digging desperately for the quote as to how he had felt, which I had been sent to get. "It must have been something pulling yourself up enough to get your leg around that chain. Did you perhaps pray, and do you think that you were saved by God?"

"No," he said, "I think I was saved because I am a very strong boy and take sitting-up exercises every morning. I don't believe in God, because I am an atheist, but don't put that in the paper because people don't like it."

That was long ago and I didn't put it in the paper because I hoped he would sell how he felt to a TV network program.

HOPE ROOT

City Edition
December 3, 1953

Hope Root, fifty-two-year-old Miami lawyer who dives for a world's record in the Gulf Stream at noon, took along enough Dramamine today to dose all his helpers and keep them from being seasick. He will make the dive in any rough water that comes, this side of a gale, he said this morning.

At five minutes past noon he expected to hold a new world's record for diving to 430 feet, or he will be dead.

There has been considerable unorganized betting on the dive among divers all over this area. Root knows the odds offered are heavily against his success.

"Bet on me," he said very quietly. "I can go down to 450 feet, but I'm going to stop at 430 feet."

Awaiting the short and stocky lawyer in the twilight blue at the bottom of his plunge may be death from nitrogen narcosis—"rapture of the great depths"—or drowning that would follow the narcosis.

He dives today to beat the record of a dead man, Maurice Fargues. Fargues wrote his name on a slate on a shotline at a depth of 396 feet, tried to go deeper, and died. His inert body was hauled to the surface with the mouthpiece of his diving apparatus hanging on his chest.

The Frenchman dived with a rope around his waist. Root dives free of all lines. If the deadly, beautiful narcosis that he recognizes as a threat kills him, his body may never be recovered.

Little is known medically of the nitrogen narcosis with which the diver flirts today. It resembles the anoxia that airplane pilots often feel when they go too high without oxygen or pressurized cabins. Other divers who have experienced it often described their ecstacy, their impaired judgment. Many divers feel it after they pass 200 feet.

Root has never felt it at all.

He has shown that he has physically a much greater margin of safety than most divers. In practice plunges in October he went to 370 feet and ended up in the mud on the bottom. His safety man who dived with him had to go back up at 200 feet because he felt the nitrogen narcosis overcoming him.

Yesterday Root said, "I think I'll get away with this because I'm short and hefty. The tall thin fellows feel the rapture of the depths first."

He weighs 170 pounds, is five feet, five inches tall. His shape may save him, says the doctor who makes the trip with Root today. He has less body surface per pound to receive the tremendous water pressure than does the tall thin man. This may have something to do with his margin of safety.

But the medical man stressed that "the greatest chance Root has in coming up to air safely again lies in the fact that he is a stable individual. Medical literature shows that such men can resist the illusions of nitrogen narcosis longest at great depths."

Steady, reflective, controlled—his friends agree that describes his temperament. But they all agree today in wishing he wouldn't dive.

The party was to leave the Terminal Docks on the MacArthur causeway at 11 A.M. They planned an hour's run to the Gulf Stream. The dive should take five minutes.

Root is diving with an aqualung and wears two tanks of compressed air. In dives where helium gas was used to replace nitrogen in the tanks, men have gone safely to greater depths than Root's 430-foot goal without narcosis. But Root is using unmixed air, and dives for that record.

He is equipped with face masks, swim fins, shirt, and shorts. Most divers must wear lead weights to overcome their buoyancy, eight to ten pounds of lead. Root is so heavy he wears no weight belt.

The dive is being made within the western edge of the Gulf Stream. A steel cable is being dropped with an anchor on the end, but the anchor doesn't reach the bottom. Along the cable, markers are tied at every 100 feet until 300 feet. Beyond that there are markers at 350 feet, 380 feet, 410 feet and 430 feet. Root hopes to swim down the cable hand over hand, tear off the marker at 430 feet, and return to the surface.

A later edition of the News that day carried a ship-to-shore telephone account of what then happened:

Aboard U-M Boat T-19 in the Gulf Stream, a fifty-two-year-old Miami attorney gambled with death in the wave-tossed waters of the Atlantic this afternoon—and apparently lost.

Hope Root, who was attempting to break the world's record for deep sea diving, entered the water at 12:27 P.M. here some four miles off Miami Beach.

He had enough compressed air in two tanks strapped to his back to stay under approximately twenty-five minutes.

Before that time ran out, it was apparent to tense observers on the surface that he was lost.

Two hours later he was presumed dead, although ships in the area continued to search for his body.

Root, a stubborn and plucky veteran of "skin diving" had been warned not to make his bid for the world's record by Reynolds, his assistant.

Moody had entered the water before Root and found that currents below were too strong to make diving feasible....

Moody stayed in the water searching for his friend and diving companion while three boats criss-crossed the area.

A Coast Guard helicopter was called to search the area.

On the scene were an eighty-three-foot Coast Guard cutter, the University of Miami's Marien Laboratory boat T-19, and the vessel Arbalete, from which Root dived.

A fresh easterly wind whipped the water to frothing whitecaps. Waves four or five feet high chopped against the boats....

▲   ▲   ▲

EDITOR'S NOTE: THE NEXT DAY'S STORY CLOSED THE RECORD OF THIS MAN'S DIVING:

December 4, 1953

Hope Root dived into the most beautiful world he knew and died in the royal blue Gulf Stream yesterday.

Somber reporters and photographers, seasick and heartsick, felt like buzzards while an awfully nice little guy went out of this world before our eyes and cameras.

We knew Root wanted it that way. But what happened after he went over the side of the ship Arbalete at 12:27 P.M. out of our sight forever? Why did he dive to death?

Part of the mystery may be cleared by pencil smudges on the graph paper, the sonic trace of Root's dive made by a fathometer. These pencil blurs seem to say this: Root went right down along the cable in a clean, even plunge, until he reached the lead weight at the bottom of the cable that was to measure his dive 400 feet below.

This plunge took him about eight minutes. Then he dived straight for the bottom beyond the cable for four minutes more.

He was alive at 550 feet when the sonic trace lost him, headed toward the mud on the bottom, 750 feet below the stainless surface.

This trace needs studying to interpret it properly, and it will be studied for days. But that was the first analysis of Lansing Wagner, University of Miami oceanographer on the marine laboratory ship that accompanied the dive ship Arbalete yesterday.

Question: The cable was 500 feet long; why did the weight on its end ride only 400 feet down? That was because the wind was blowing so hard against the ship above that the cable hung down from it at almost a 45-degree angle.

How can we say Root was alive at 530 feet, in his second inexplicable plunge beyond the cable toward the bottom? Wagner says this sonic trace is a record of the echoes from Root's air bubbles, as he went down. The aqualung used for the dive bubbles furiously only when its wearer breathes.

The moment Root lost consciousness, his mouthpiece fell out of his mouth, the bubbles stopped, the trace stopped. Evidence of other dives indicates that.

The trace lost Root in the blur of lines that are made by the sonic echo from the bottom of the ocean floor. What happened to Root's mind down there?

Did nitrogen narcosis blur his judgment and cause him to make his second plunge, beyond the cable, without removing one single marker from the line to show how far he had come?

We'll never know but we remember:

The tiny beads of sweat on his upper lip;

His eyes and the set of his lips, signalling he was locked in the grip of a great apprehension—or was it anticipation?

The dead tone in his voice; in his gentle and confiding words, no ring, no resonance.

Root dived with an aqualung two or three days a week last summer, every moment he could tear away from his law practice. Call it his sport. But when he talked of diving he talked as a man talks of his true love, his true church.

Do you think he was crazy to literally find a heaven down under the water? You ought to go and look. There isn't anything ugly down there. Everything's quiet, every movement is smooth, every color is quite perfect. On down there is just one color, the perfect blue of evening.

You can go down into that world and live for a while in your eyes, be completely satisfied just to look. You are cradled, weightless, down there in the home all life on this earth came from.

Everybody who's lucky has dreamed sometime of flying. Of soaring free. Root wouldn't wear a rope. He soared down like your dream when he dived, into perfect beauty.

Do you think he was stupid? Root was an intelligent lawyer. He had the manuscript of a good book on spear fishing in South Florida almost finished. Nobody who went out in those three boats with the man yesterday can seriously think he staged a big show to commit suicide. But everybody knew before he went over the side at 12:27 P.M. that he wasn't diving for anything so trite as a few added feet on a world's record.

Divers know what his death was like: A long plunge through beauty, ecstasy—that would be the nitrogen narcosis—blank, the end. Gone for sure, but no body, no burial, no coffin.

He was magnetized, polarized toward that dive, nothing could deflect him. But don't blame anybody, don't blame him. Don't think if something or another had been different, he might be here today. If you can't feel

27
▲

it, all the words of the psychologists won't make it any clearer.

The same voice seemed to be in him that was in Thomas Wolfe, when Wolfe wrote his only poem, just before he died of pneumonia:

Something has spoken to me in the night,
Burning the tapers of the waning year;
Something has spoken in the night,
And told me I shall die, I know not where.
Saying:
'To lose the earth you know, for greater knowing
To lose the life you have, for greater life;
To leave the friends you loved, for greater loving;
To find a land more kind than home, more large than earth

Fifty-two-year-old Hope Root was helpless yesterday in the grip of a strange, big passion. He had to dive—and die.

▲ ▲ ▲

The morning that story came out the elevator operator said, "I know what you mean, Jane."

The day after a letter in Spencerian handwriting came to me:

Dear Jane Wood,

Please come to see me. I am Hope Root's mother. You wrote about him as though you had known him always.

Sincerely,
Cynthia Hope Root

When I went to see her she told me she was eighty years old. She asked me to see that a little book Hope was writing got published. I did. It's a good little book, never enough promoted. The title: *Skindiving and Spearfishing on the Florida Reefs*. In the preface he wrote:

"I have goggle-fished almost from the beginning in Miami—1938. I have done tower diving as a sport on the side and was with Pete Desjardins' water show one year.

"I believe in good physical condition and continually fight tendencies in myself to overindulge in anything except goggle-fishing. I succeed only fairly well."

Hope had set an unofficial record before, on November 27, 1953. He had reached a depth of 350 feet. Paul Arnold was the only witness to that feat, although Ed Fisher above them took underwater photographs of the deep dive. Ed later camped out underwater for twenty-four hours, and I did the world's first underwater interview, as far as I know. You interview underwater by writing on a slate with a slate pencil.

To Ed, after about fifteen hours, I wrote, "Think you can make it?"

Ed wrote back, "I can make it."

He did.

Once in the 1950s when I went into the dive shop to rent some air tanks, Ed Parnell said to me, "Jane, you have done so much for scuba diving I would like to give you free air as long as I work in the shop."

I thought about it. Knew some newspaper writers were on the take. Then I thought if I were ever asked, "Were you ever on the take?" I could honestly answer:

"Yeah, I took free air."

I did, about forty dollars worth that summer, until Ed quit to become a school teacher.

MIAMI - 1920 TO 1950

That gutsy city, Miami, made it through the war and happily welcomed more tourists afterward. Three hurricanes in 1947 and two in 1948 didn't help in the welcome. Though they were not very severe, they wer... wet. They ... much rain ... that Mia... national A... under a few... water for m... nd western... ounty was fl... ys. Henry ha... r cows in th... ause the w... igh he coul... under the... ws have... ed regularly (... dries up.)... he Miami lif... which folks had... for three decades... change dramati-... in 1950. U.S.... Estes Kefauver... the Senate... Committee to... ate Crime to... n May 1950.... staged one of... evealing crime... here. He got... lter Clark of

Broward to admit over radio at the hearing that he was a partner in bolita business. Many Miamians will never forget the dramatic moment when, fear oozing from his voice, Sheriff Cl...

High point of the comedy was the appearance of a little Miami Beach bookie named Frenchie Gips who leaped from his bed in bathrobe and carpet slippers to tell all to Kefauver and the radio audience in a hilarious performance.

Kefauver rubbed the noses of Miamians in the gambl...

Nobody could squinch their eyes shut any more at the enormous graft in illegal bookmaking. The grand jury indicted just about everybody in sight in the gambling ... riff ... of ... n, ... general as sheriff in 1952 on a platform that was nothing but opposition to illegal gambling. Sheriff Kelly made his name and fame by raiding bookies.

There was still a prostitution ring on Miami Beach, with taxi drivers acting as pimps for call girls. There were still bookies operating on

▲ FLORIDA: ON THE EDGE
OF PEACE AND MYSTERY ▼

MIAMI 1920 TO 1950

HURRICANE

THE BEST WE COULD

CORAL GABLES

XANADU

TIMBER

CORAL GABLES

A massive man who could sell because he was s vince because he was convinced, built Coral Gable George Merrick.

They are celebrating the twenty-fifth annive town starting today, and they are saying that ar the place is the history of George Merrick.

They think he did a good job.

He was unique in an era that produced so gaudy figures. He built a town that has a speci Merrick and his city had great good luck in outstanding virtues and avoiding the outst the wildest era this area has ever known—

of the 1920's.

century since the to

there th

HURRICANE

The worst hurricane ever to hit land in the world swirled in upon the Florida Keys twenty years ago on the evening of September 2, 1935. Small in diameter, the core of the storm was wrapped with winds blowing 250 miles an hour. The winds lifted one great wave that to a lighthouse keeper "looked ninety feet high," and rolled that wave over a handful of small islands to drown more than four hundred people who had nowhere to go to get away. That wave twisted railroad tracks thirty feet above the sea. Houses disintegrated, and the leaves were stripped from the tough many-rooted mangrove trees that never blow over. Years later and miles away, skeletons of some of the ninety people missing after the storm were still being found among the mangrove roots. Edney Captain Parker, his wife, and ten of his children were washed to sea that night, and they all lived, and were not much hurt. They lived to see in the days that followed something worse than the black inferno of this hurricane's heart. They lived through a white hell, with the stench of the bodies of their dead

▲ Photo on previous spread: Using her oars as tent poles, Jane Wood Reno sets up camp on the beach. Always an outdoors person, Jane spent much of her life exploring the mysteries of Florida's wilderness areas.

MIAMI
1920 TO 1950

When we left north Georgia in 1925 and came to Miami to live, my family was leaving a land with an economy blighted by the boll weevil for a bayside city enjoying a fantastic boom. The traffic to Miami on the old Dixie Highway was worse than anything in rush hour today.

Downtown Miami was exciting, I discovered. The city had really become itself—jubilant, high of heart, wild. Binder boys, dressed in knickerbockers, thronged Flagler Street, selling their "binders"—options to buy land—to people who hoped to double their money in a few weeks. The port of Miami was crowded with ships, including five-masted sailing ships and freighters of all sizes. They were helping the railroad bring building materials to Miami.

But I thought that on the whole Miami was dumb, dull, and flat. I had loved the pines and oaks of north Georgia, and those I saw around Miami were shrimps. I had loved going barefoot in the summer in the soft red clay dust of my homeland's hills, but the grass along the beaches down here had sandspurs. I was twelve years old.

My contempt for Miami was blown away on September 18, 1926. Actually, my love affair with south Florida began the evening before. We were living in a rented house on Collins Avenue and Fourteenth Street on Miami Beach, a block from the ocean. Mother and I walked down to the beach in the late afternoon to admire the most beautiful sunset we had ever seen. High-flying cirrus clouds and widespread cumulus floated across the sky from east to west. Everything was gold and pink and blue and calm.

It was a classic hurricane sunset, well known to meteorologists. Later, after my love affair with this part of the world began, I was to find out that Father B. Venes had in writing of hurricane sunsets in 1898 said, "The ruby color is gradually turning into crimson as the sun is reaching the horizon, and shortly after its setting the whole sky has the appearance of an enormous conflagration...."

It was the morning after that sunset that I fell in love. At 7 A.M. my mother shook me and said, "Wake up, Jane! There has been a terrible hurricane!" I sat up in bed and said, "Why didn't you wake me up?" She said, "It's over now!" I ran to the window and looked out. The sky was a clear and beautiful blue. There was not enough wind to blow out a candle. Miami Beach was covered by more than thirty inches of water. Cars were wrapped around fire plugs. Was I thrilled!

Daddy was asleep on a sofa, and the younger kids were asleep on the dirty clothes in the dirty clothes closet. Those were the only dry places in the house. The windows had been blown out on two sides of the house. Mother and Uncle Roy and I put on our bathing suits and waded four blocks to a friend's apartment, Blanch Kell, to see how she fared. A big, tired snapper was swimming slowly down Michigan Avenue, four blocks from the ocean. We took him home to dinner.

So many newcomers to Miami did not know that this was the lull in the eye of the hurricane. Then it hit again! The winds blew away the wind gauges after registering 138 miles an hour. Gusts were later registered at up to 200 miles an hour. Mother decided to stay at Blanch's apartment. My uncle and I walked home together, holding hands, leaning against the wind, grinning at each other. Nothing blew off and hit us. I loved it so! There is something in the heart of a thirteen-year-old that loves vandalism.

There was plenty of excitement besides hurricanes, but I didn't know about it then. There were wide-open whore houses all over town throughout the twenties and thirties. It was generally understood by everybody, including law enforcement folks, that they were needed to keep the tourist industry going. The most esteemed of such establishments was Gertie Walsh's whore house in an old stone mansion built in 1903 on Flagler Street.

"You have never seen anything so stunning as Gertie, all 250 pounds of her, and her sister Blanch, all 200 pounds of her, coming down the stairs of the old Brigham mansion, dressed in pink satin, with ostrich plume feathers," my late husband once told me.

Henry had student rates, until, at age thirty-six, he married me. He was a *Miami Herald* reporter. "Nice women think they can tell a whore, but Gertie's girls were perfectly beautiful," he said.

I never really believed him until, years later, Mrs. Whitie told me of Gertie's girls. "In the early twenties," she remembered, "I had a dress shop downtown on Flagler Street. I used to outfit Gertie's girls. Of course, I wouldn't ask any of the girls who worked for me to wait on them. Gertie brought them in after the shop was closed.

"Jane," she said, "they were as beautiful as Maggy and Kay."

Maggy, my daughter, and Kay, her granddaughter, were fifteen then. I thereafter believed what I had heard about Gertie's girls.

In the early thirties Miami had one of its sporadic attacks of law enforcement, and the whore houses around the town were closed. They were allowed to open again not too long afterward and Gertie rented a house in the Miami River, the first whore house in this area with a yacht basin. It was opposite the Police Benevolent Association playground.

Henry told me about what went on in the yacht basin. One night as he was leaving the house, Gertie said to him, "Henry, I know you majored in agriculture and I want to ask you something. I sent a couple of the girls downtown to buy two flamingos, and they called back and said, 'Gertie, they want five hundred dollars each.'

"I told them to buy swans, and they called back and said, 'They want five hundred dollars each for the swans.' I told them to come home.

"Then Blanch and I read an ad in the paper saying, *Ducks, catch them yourself. $1.00.* So Blanch and I put on straw hats and borrowed a truck from some workmen who were working here and went out and caught ducks. And they have been here for months and none of them have laid any eggs."

She took him out beside the yacht basin and showed him those red-headed Muscovy ducks swimming around. He looked them over thoughtfully and said "Gertie, you caught all males."

Not long ago I asked Allen Morris whatever happened to Gertie Walsh. He said that she ran a whore house in Jacksonville for a number of years, and died about fifteen years ago.

"After I was married, Gertie never would let me get in bed with one of her girls. But when I came through Jacksonville she would let me spend the night sleeping on a cot in her kitchen," he said.

▲   ▲   ▲

I knew the stately stone mansion as Peg Brigham's home. Her father and mother built it in 1903, when Peg was two years old. The Brigham's son Ed was born there. It was built on forty acres that they owned that stretched from Flagler Street to the Miami River. One night when Ed was a little boy, a panther stuck his head through the window of the living room and looked around. Ed and his father sat very still, and the panther finally went away.

Mrs. Brigham made a lot of money in real estate in the early twenties, but she didn't have much after the big boom busted in 1926. The family, receiving no rent, had to move back in their old home when Gertie had to move out of the house in the early thirties.

Peg was one of the great, the wonderful, people of the world—kind, wise, generous, brilliant. She wrote fine prose, though she never finished anything or published any of her writing.

"I spoiled Sister," Mrs. Brigham once told me. "I gave her fifty dollars a day spending money when she was eighteen."

When Peg no longer had money with which to help friends, her strength and kindness were still there. She could listen to a friend's problems and find a good solution. She returned you to yourself feeling your very best, polished like a silver spoon. Her eyes had the sparkle of true beauty. Married five times, she died a baroness.

The second time I talked to Peg after I met her, I came to her house and asked her mother if she was at home.

"She's upstairs in bed, not feeling well," said Mrs. Brigham, indicating that I could go up.

When I went into her bedroom, she was propped up in a bed like Sarah Bernhardt dying of consumption, and I said, "What's the matter, Peg?"

"I have been to Ludlow Fair."

"What does that mean?"

She replied,

> "I have been to Ludlow Fair
> And left my necktie God knows where
> Carried halfway home, or near
> Pints and quarts of Ludlow beer.
>
> Down in lovely mud I've lain,
> Happy 'til I walked again.
> The world it was the old world yet,
> I was I, my things were wet

And nothing now remains to do
But begin the game anew."

Then she said, "I was drunk."

She had a problem of getting drunk and doing things like falling in the Roney Plaza pool and being arrested for simple drunkenness.

Peg died young, in her forties, in the forties. She left two fine sons. She died of cancer and was in a Catholic hospital for three months before her death. There she became converted to Catholicism.

By then the old Brigham mansion was a funeral home, and Peg was buried from the living room. There were many, many people at her funeral service. Among the pallbearers in the first row were my husband, several judges, and others who remembered this room as the parlor of Gertie Walsh's whore house, I knew. Peg was propped up in her open casket, looking like she had been to Ludlow Fair. The whole scene incensed me, and I felt that if Peg were not dead she would die in sheer disgust.

A Catholic priest came out and chanted many lines in Latin as he walked around the casket. Then he concluded: "Take her to Paradise, her native home, and may the Angels greet her!"

We who loved her wept with happiness. It was the perfect epitaph.

▲   ▲   ▲

Throughout the 1920s it was dangerous to be on Biscayne Bay in a small boat at night. There would be rumrunners racing up the bay loaded with the booze, who were being chased by hijackers who were shooting at them, and who were being chased by Coast Guard boats who were shooting at both.

They ran hard liquor in from the Bahamas and Cuba and they made moonshine in the Everglades. They took the booze north from Miami in cars with springs reinforced so that the body of the car wouldn't sag with the weight of the load. Miami was the principal source of most of the bootleg liquor sold in the eastern part of the United States during Prohibition.

Years after Prohibition was repealed, a grey-haired captain on a tugboat told me:

"I came to Miami in 1923 from up around Cedar Key. I got me a fast little boat with a thirty-horse motor. It wouldn't hold more than about twenty, thirty cases of whiskey, but it would outrun anything the Coast Guard had. A bunch of us had boats like that and we were running whiskey in from Bimini to Miami. We came through Bear Cut, and the Coast Guard knew what we were doing, and we knew that they knew, but they couldn't catch us.

"So, one nice afternoon there were maybe twenty of us over in Bimini, and we knew the Coast Guard was waiting. But we decided to run for it. They could only catch one, if any.

"We hit Bear Cut about dusk, and there was the Coast Guard cutter, and we tore past. Well, they had stretched a cable across the Cut, a foot or so under water. We hit it and you should have seen the scrambled boats! Wrecked, sunk! Nobody killed, and it was a wonder. But for some reason, I don't know why, I hit that cable and it swung so that it lifted me up and over, and I was on through! No damage at all. I got out of that business then. You don't have to have something that lucky happen twice."

▲ ▲ ▲

The belle of Amherst lived in Coconut Grove in the early twenties, and some of Emily Dickinson's finest poems, unpublished, floated in a camphor-wood chest in Coconut Grove after the 1926 hurricane. Some people who saw a silly musical play on Miami Beach a few years ago may think the belle of Amherst was Emily Dickinson. Certainly Emily was the most wonderful poet America has ever produced, but the belle of Amherst was her editor-translator, Mabel Loomis Todd.

Mrs. Todd spent years in Amherst, at the request of Emily's sister Lavinia, poring over a jumble of words on odds and ends of paper at a task that sometimes looked impossible. She edited, with a little help from Thomas Wentworth Higginson, three volumes of Emily's poems and a volume of her letters.

At the same time she was the mistress of a very rich, very obliging millionaire, Arthur Curtis James. Mrs. Todd was married to a professor of astronomy who taught at Amherst College. Mr. James took Dr. and Mrs. Todd to Japan on his yacht once, because Dr. Todd wanted to observe an eclipse of the sun there.

After the first three volumes of poems and the letters were published, Mrs. Todd stopped her editing work in the late 1890s because of a row between her and certain members of Emily's family. It was said that there was a romance going on between her and Emily's brother, Austin. The remaining undeciphered poems she had been given she locked in a camphor-wood chest.

When Dr. Todd retired from Amherst in 1917, Mr. James gave him and his wife a house in Coconut Grove, a cottage just north of Main Highway. It was near Mr. James's mansion beside Biscayne Bay.

In the 1926 hurricane the Todd's home was partly demolished, flooded, and the contents water-damaged. The camphor-wood chest that held the remaining manuscripts floated and Emily's poems didn't get wet. Mrs. Todd moved away from Miami. In 1929 she asked her daughter, Millicent Todd Bingham, to open the chest. Mrs. Bingham published the poems she found in 1945, in a book she entitled *Bolts of Melody*. Lovers of Emily's poems can only say, "Lord bless camphor-wood, as well as Mrs. Todd and Mrs. Bingham."

▲   ▲   ▲

In 1925, for the first time, hotels in Miami stayed open from July through September. Before that they had been closed during those months. That winter Miami offered entertainment fare as fine as any metropolis in the nation. Mme. Galli-Curci sang and Flo Ziegfeld performed at the Royal Palm Hotel. Paderewski played the piano there. Paul Whiteman played at the Coral Gables Country Club, and Chaliapin sang at the Biltmore Hotel.

The Venetian causeway between Miami and Miami Beach opened early in 1926. But the boom was beginning to slow down early that year. The channel entering Miami's harbor was blocked when a ship, the *Prins Valdemar*, sank there. The railroad had problems. Only infrequently could building materials be brought to the booming city.

Many newcomers headed north after the hurricane, for the city was really a shambles, the boom had really busted. Too many Miamians suffered from hunger for some years. All but one of the banks failed. Four acres of land and a home in South Miami that sold for $40,000 in 1924 sold for $900 on a tax deed in 1929.

In that severe depression many who could eat had no money for movies or anything like that. At that time a fifteen-year-old friend was hit by that passion for culture that overcomes many of us in the full flood of adolescence. He sat down and learned the title of all the volumes of the encyclopedia: "A to Anno," "Anno to Baltic," "Baltic to Brail," and so on, clear through to "Vase to Zygo."

In spite of the depression which came to Miami before it hit the rest of the country, some fine things happened here in the late 1920s.

The Cardboard College, also known as the University of Miami, opened in 1926 in Coral Gables. A dream of George Merrick, it was housed in a half-finished hotel with walls of cardboard until after World War II. When it first opened professors were paid in scrip for many months, and lived from hand to mouth. The scrip was accepted by some stores in Coral Gables.

Dr. Bowman Foster Ashe was the first president of the college. He made it live because he could inspire professors and students alike to do their very best. It was the attentive, believing, open-hearted way that he listened to people.

The university gave working scholarships to many students. Parents were allowed to sign notes, payable over a lengthy period, for tuition. Many Miamians who could not have attended any other college got an excellent education there in the Great Depression.

In the 1930s the university's Winter Institute of Literature was created. It brought some fine writers, such as poets Robert Frost and Padriac Colum, to teach. Molly Colum, a great literary critic, conducted a course in the modern novel. She had a most beautiful speaking voice and was an inspiration to her classes.

The University of Miami spawned the Miami Symphony Orchestra. It was created in the 1930s by Dr. Arnold Volpe, a professor of music at the university. Internationally famous stars appeared with the orchestra. The first concerts were held in the auditorium of Miami Senior High School.

Plenty of illegal gambling was going on all over town in the twenties. There were slot machines that took dimes in grocery stores. What is today the fishing pier on south Miami Beach had an elegant gambling casino on it. The casino was complete with roulette wheels, faro, dice tables, blackjack, and striptease artists.

Police had other problems. A policeman friend once told me that one night he and a buddy were patrolling in a police car and drove into a golf course on what had once been the old Sewall estate, just west of Jackson Memorial Hospital. The two friends had been fishing together all night the night before and they wanted to take a nap.

They were driving in on a little dirt road when they suddenly heard a scream that sounded like, "Help! Help! Help!" The driver speeded up, and the other officer pulled out his pistol. They reached a tall pine tree beside the road when they heard the screams again from the top of the tree.

"That's the first woman I ever heard being raped in a tree top," said one of the officers.

There were peacocks on what had been an old estate, and it was mating season, the season when peacocks scream.

▲　　▲　　▲

In one of the first acts of Congress in 1933 after Franklin D. Roosevelt became president, the Prohibition Act was repealed. Liquor became legal again. The bootleggers and rumrunners switched to illegal gambling. In the thirties gambling spread and spread.

Before Repeal, nice Coral Gables ladies made home brew for their husbands, even if neither they nor their husbands liked the taste of the stuff. It was the thing to do, like being a member of the D.A.R. After Repeal they went to the races, or to an illegal bookie parlor occasionally in the afternoon.

There were bookie joints all over the place and bolita tickets were sold everywhere. There were little gambling parlors in the heart of downtown Miami where addicts could play poker and blackjack with professionals for high stakes.

The Embassy Club on NE Second Avenue was a swank gambling casino patronized by top society until February 27, 1932, when it was held up by five bandits. One was killed. The dead bandit had a wooden arm. That holdup ended all illegal gambling in Miami quite briefly.

Al Capone first came to Miami in 1928, and later the nationally famous gangster bought a home on Palm Island and spent the winters there. It was said that he had the best cook in Florida, which may have been why no one refused to dine at Al's. He entertained numerous important politicians and syndicated columnist Damon Runyon, among others.

Sheriff Dan Hardie lived at one end of the same island. Sippi Morris lived in a rented garage apartment nearby. Sippi had a pet raccoon that occasionally went over and scooped goldfish from a small goldfish pond in Capone's yard. Sippi lived in fear until Capone went north again that year.

Governor Carlton tried to have Capone officially declared "undesirable" to the state and have him put out of his residence. Vincent Giblin, Capone's lawyer, successfully defended the gangster's right to live on Palm Island. Capone got into the rackets around Miami. He was jailed by the federal government for income tax evasion in the thirties and sent to Alcatraz prison in San Francisco Bay. Giblin became a Dade County circuit court judge in the 1950s.

Red Rainwater, Frank Hyde, Red Slaton, Big Sam Cohen, Jules Levitt, Charlie Friedman—those were among the unemployed bootleggers who rose to head gambling syndicates. Hyde and Slaton headed the first big bookie empire that shaped up in Hialeah in the early 1930s. Hyde became Dade County agent for Moe Annenberg, head of the nation's race wire service. He peddled the race result information to smaller bookies and had about twenty subagents.

Telephones supplied the lifelines of the bookie organization. By 1935, the bookie racket headed by Hyde and Slaton had become a $30,000,000 a year business. Law enforcement officials tried to cripple it by taking away the telephones, but Judge Jefferson B. Browne ordered the Southern Bell Telephone and Telegraph Company to furnish telephone service to Hyde in 1936. Hyde's lawyer, Vincent Giblin, won this historic decision by arguing that though his client admitted he was a bookmaker, a common carrier (the phone company) is not a defender of the public morals.

There were few defenders of the public morals for two decades. Dan Hardie, Dade County Sheriff in 1932-1933, closed the town to gambling and drove to enforce the gambling laws. For this he was removed by Governor Dave Sholtz on the grounds he showed faulty judgment. Most of the town was against Hardie's drive. It was a depression decade. Miamians thought they had to have gambling to attract winter tourists.

Hyde and Slaton were squeezed out in the late 1930s to make room for a group of younger men who formed what came to be known as the Miami Syndicate. Eddie Padgett, Merle Yarborough, Bill Bartlett, and Ace Deuce Solomon were among that powerful group. On the Miami Beach side of the bay the powerful S & G Syndicate took shape. Jules Levitt, Harold Salvey, Sam Cohen, Jack Friedlander, and Eddie Rosenbloom began as rivals, leasing concessions of cigar stands from Miami Beach hotels for their horse-booking. They combined into the S & G (which didn't stand for anything) in the early 1940s, and branched out into table gambling.

By the end of the 1940s, the S & G was a slick monopoly that took in $100,000,000 a year in bets, paid out an estimated million a year in bribes to law enforcement officers, big and small.

While all this was happening, the local laws made one boast—that gambling here was run by "hometown boys." It wasn't much of a boast, since a number of the hometown boys had killings on their records. But after the end of the war they could make it no longer. The nation's mobs moved in. Remnants of Al Capone's crew, the Purple Gang of Detroit, and Murder, Inc. opened up in Dade County. Broward County was more wide open than Dade. Around the dice tables fellows with fists full of bills from easy wartime profits stood three-deep to lose their money. Harry Russell, an Al Capone lieutenant, muscled into the S & G syndicate with the help of some timely raids by state investigators.

Police departments and the sheriff's office were riddled with corruption. The fellow who collected tribute to pay police was called "The Ice Man." The

S & G had its own crop of private detectives, called "beards," who watched the little bookies to see they did not hold back bets from the big boys.

What were the good people of Dade and Broward doing all this time? They were sitting with their eyes squinched as tight shut as they could squinch them. Both Miami newspapers exposed the situation, describing how and where illegal gambling was operating. The gamblers laughed and called the stories good advertising.

▲　▲　▲

Crazy political violence came to Miami in February, 1933. President-elect Roosevelt was speaking in Bayfront Park auditorium. Mayor Anton Cermak of Chicago was on the podium with him. Guiseppi Sangara got up, shot, and killed Cermak. Roosevelt was not hurt. The assassin was apparently a lone, deranged creature and was executed not long thereafter.

In 1935 flowers were dropped by airplane over Bayfront Park during a memorial service attended by thousands for those who died in the Labor Day hurricane that hit Islamorada on the Florida Keys. It was the worst hurricane ever to hit land in the western world at that time. Hundreds of jobless war veterans had been brought there by the federal government to work on an overseas highway to Key West. Most were killed, except the ones who had come up to Miami because it was payday weekend. The weather forecasting had been terrible.

There were lots of losers living in Miami in the thirties, people who lost jobs, couldn't find others, and went hungry. Roosevelt's Federal Emergency Relief Administration helped some, to some extent, but not much.

Along North Miami Avenue, the principal residents were aging prostitutes and unemployed Cuban cigar makers. The Cubans, among the wave of refugees that came over in 1898, finally found ways to get over to Tampa where they might find jobs making cigars. The aging prostitutes would make do on two dollars a week from the FERA. WPA workers in a federal project for the unemployed did some fine things. The coral rock structures around Matheson Hammock Park and Matheson Beach are their handiwork.

Even the people who didn't go hungry were mostly low on money. A friend remembers: "It was sort of fun, everybody being broke together. The Grove had a sense of community. There was no breaking and entering, nobody locked doors."

▲　▲　▲

43
▲

In the summer of 1937 Amelia Earhart decided to fly east around the world, instead of west. The city desk of the Miami Herald learned that she was to land most unexpectedly on a Sunday afternoon at Opa-Locka airport. There was no one in the city room but the assistant city editor and me, so he had to send me.

She was so beautiful, her green eyes so responsive! And she was so patient with the aging photographer from the *Miami Tribune* who spent ten minutes telling her all about his flying experience before I could ask a question.

"Why are you flying around the world, Miss Earhart?" I asked.

"What do you mean, 'Why?'" she asked.

"Is it just for fun? Or is there a scientific purpose?"

She reflected and said, "Yes, just for fun."

She took off from Miami with her navigator, Fred Noonan, in June, and they went down in the Pacific on July 2, 1937. Reverence fills my heart when I hear the song, "Happy landings to thee, Amelia Earhart. Farewell first lady of the air!"

▲   ▲   ▲

Tourism increased throughout the thirties. Miami's basic commodity for visitors had always been sunshine. Some attractions were added. For instance, the old wrecked ship *Prins Valdemar* that had been washed up beside Biscayne Boulevard was converted to an aquarium with snakes on top. It was a great place to learn to tell the difference between a poisonous water moccasin and a harmless black water snake. Look into their eyes. The poisonous snake has pupils that are a vertical slit. The harmless snake has round pupils.

But Miami's sale of sunshine stopped after February 1942. Germany sent submarines to the Gulf Stream to torpedo ships carrying crude rubber and oil north to East Coast ports. A blackout was ordered for Miami and Miami Beach. We could see smoke from burning tankers from the tops of tall buildings along Biscayne Boulevard.

My sister Dolly's husband, Bill Denslow, was among the men who went out in small boats and salvaged bales of crude rubber to sell, before he was drafted. The Army Air Force took over many Miami Beach hotels for training quarters for Corps enlisted men and officers. Gertie Walsh's whore house on the Miami River was closed, as were all the others.

A huge dirigible was sent by the U.S. Navy to south Florida to scout for German submarines. It was housed in a hangar in south Dade County at Richmond base until it was shot down by a submarine as it flew over the Gulf

Stream. The hangar burned in a hurricane in 1945, because many small planes had been put in it to protect them from the storm. Today the old base is the site of the new Metro Zoo.

▲   ▲   ▲

That gutsy city, Miami, made it through the war and happily welcomed more tourists afterward. Three hurricanes in 1947 and two in 1948 didn't help in the welcome. Though they were not very severe, they were very wet. They brought so much rain with them that Miami International Airport was under a few inches of water for many hours and western Dade County was flooded for days. Henry had to milk our cows in the water, because the water was so high he couldn't set a pail under the cows. (Cows have to be milked regularly or their milk dries up.)

The Miami life-style with which folks had lived for three decades was to change dramatically in 1950. U.S. Senator Estes Kefauver brought the Senate Special Committee to Investigate Crime to Miami in May 1950. Kefauver staged one of his most revealing crime hearings here. He got Sheriff Walter Clark of Broward to admit over radio at the hearing that he was a partner in bolita business. Many Miamians will never forget the dramatic moment when, fear oozing from his voice, Sheriff Clark made the reluctant confession to Kefauver.

Sheriff Jimmy Sullivan of Dade fared much better before the gangling senator. Sullivan, a long-winded and rambling talker anyway, filibustered like a senator. He talked and talked and said nothing and was so boring he slowed Kefauver's show and left the stand without any damaging admissions about anything.

High point of the comedy was the appearance of a little Miami Beach bookie named Frenchie Gips who leaped from his bed in bathrobe and carpet slippers to tell all to Kefauver and the radio audience in a hilarious performance.

Kefauver rubbed the noses of Miamians in the gambling dirt. Nobody could squinch their eyes shut any more at the enormous graft in illegal book-making. The grand jury indicted just about everybody in sight in the gambling world, including Sheriff Sullivan and a host of deputies. The indictments fell down, because many of them were based on the testimony of a self-confessed perjurer. With all the tremendous hullabaloo, not one person went to jail.

But the community felt badly shamed. There was a profound public revulsion, and that revulsion elected Tom Kelly, a National Guard brigadier general as sheriff in 1952 on a platform that was nothing but opposition to illegal gambling. Sheriff Kelly made his name and fame by raiding bookies.

There was still a prostitution ring on Miami Beach, with taxi drivers acting as pimps for call girls. There were still bookies operating on the sneak, but there was little money in it when they had to sneak. There were some moonshine operations, mostly selling in the Negro section. Unorganized violence was to become more of a problem than organized corruption.

Though it had a few flaws, Miami was a wonderful place in which to grow up and raise kids in those years. Adlai Stevenson said it best. He was speaking in Bayfront Park auditorium at noon in his campaign for the presidency in 1952.

When he was a boy his grandfather brought him on his first visit to Miami, and it was a sleepy little town then, he said. Then he looked up Biscayne Boulevard and his eyes and voice lifted with delight as he said:

"You have built a splendid city, shining in the sun!"

Hurricane

The worst hurricane ever to hit land in the world swirled in upon the Florida Keys twenty years ago on the evening of September 2, 1935. Small in diameter, the core of the storm was wrapped with winds blowing 250 miles an hour. The winds lifted one great wave that to a lighthouse keeper "looked ninety feet high," and rolled that wave over a handful of small islands to drown more than four hundred people who had nowhere to go to get away.

That wave twisted railroad tracks thirty feet above the sea. Houses disintegrated, and the leaves were stripped from the tough many-rooted mangrove trees that never blow over. Years later and miles away, skeletons of some of the ninety people missing after the storm were still being found among the mangrove roots.

Captain Edney Parker, his wife, and ten of his children were washed to sea that night, and they all lived, and were not much hurt. They lived to see in the days that followed something worse than the black inferno of this hurricane's heart. They lived through a white hell, with the stench of the bodies of their dead friends rising from among the dead mangroves. Before the end of that September week that began with a hurricane warning (the same week when Captain Parker burned those bodies in ghastly pyres at Islamorada), Captain Parker found himself looking down a pistol barrel at a National Guardsman and wondering if he would be making a mistake if he didn't shoot the man.

When hurricane warnings went up on Monday morning, Captain Parker, a lean, brown veteran of six hurricanes, didn't worry. He was born in Key West in 1887, and his daddy moved the family to Plantation Key to farm when he was a nipper. Later, they homesteaded on Upper Matecumbe, where they raised sugar sop, sour apples, tomatoes, cabbages, watermelons, pineapples, sweet peppers. One hurricane young Edney spent raiding a watermelon patch.

He had been in the 1906 storm that drowned four hundred of Henry Flagler's railroad workers when they were taking the trains to sea as they built the great trestles from the Florida mainland to Key West.

But compared with what was bearing down on him that Labor Day, every other storm had been a gentle little zephyr.

Five feet, straight as a ramrod and not much fatter was Captain Parker. But nobody on the Keys doubted that he was quite some man. He could be trusted with a boat and a gun. A charter boat captain, he knew the hole on Alligator Reef where all the barracudas lie waiting to bite anything that flashes past. A constable, he was as much law as his Key needed. Father of eleven children, he was on the school board.

In his voice was that clear British accent and that West Indian lilt, so surprising to visitors to the Keys when they first meet the native fishermen of those islands, the "Conchs." A century ago the Bahamas were in the background of these people, who seem as much citizens of the southern sea around them as they are of the U.S.A.

None of Captain Parker's Conch neighbors were fooled by the fact that he was a little thin man with a gentle voice. They had the habit of entrusting leadership, in the rare instances when they wanted any, to Captain Parker. He was a personage on the Florida Keys.

In that faraway depression summer of 1935, Captain Parker was working for the veterans camps of the FERA. The bonus marchers of 1932, Hoover's administration, had wound up on the Florida Keys in 1935. The veterans of World War I who had marched on Washington at the bottom of the depression were fat and sassy on the Keys that Labor Day. They had faced Douglas MacArthur on a white horse when he rode against them under Herbert Hoover's order. But they had not been able to resist New Deal blandishments.

Roosevelt's FERA had set up three tent camps between Snake Creek and Lower Matecumbe, on the Florida Keys. There the veterans ate three huge meals of steak, crawfish, chicken, and ice cream every day. They fished, piddled along at building a highway to Key West, and got thirty dollars a month pay. In more than a year the highway they were working on had become visible, but barely so. It reached about two hundred feet into the water. They were good men who only got drunk once a month, because they only got paid once a month.

Labor Day weekend was payday weekend and more than half the 716 veterans on the Keys had taken off for a baseball game in Miami. Captain Parker was very glad of that, when he heard Monday morning that a hurricane was whirling somewhere offshore.

Before dawn that day, Grady Norton, head of the U.S. weather bureau's hurricane warning service in Jacksonville, called Fred Ghent, the commander of the state's veteran's camps, who was also in Jacksonville. Norton told Ghent a hurricane might threaten the Florida Keys that day. Ghent set the year-old plan for evacuating the veterans to the mainland into motion. He called Ray Sheldon, his subordinate, and chief of the camps on the Keys.

"Call for the train," Ghent said, "when it looks like the hurricane is going to hit the Keys."

So Sheldon, at Islamorada headquarters on Upper Matecumbe, got on the phone to Miami, and all that morning everybody on the party line picked up the receiver and listened every time he talked to the Miami weather bureau. They played poker at headquarters in Captain Ed Butters's hotel, while they waited on that most fatal holiday.

And they talked about what a job it would be to round up the weekending veterans, who had been spending their monthly paychecks, if it did look like the hurricane was going to hit. Plans were all made to camp at Hollywood, north of Miami—"and will that be a mess!"

At 12:15 P.M., Sheldon told Captain Parker, "Call for the train!"

And the little captain did call to tell the Florida East Coast Railroad to send the train that was supposed to be made up and waiting in Homestead, fifty miles north.

That afternoon Captain Parker spent helping tie things down at the camp on Snake Creek, before he started home. Then he climbed into a truck, picked up his 240-pound son-in-law, Jack Ryder. He had a fifty-gallon drum of insecticide in the back of the truck. As they crossed Whale Harbor fill, a gust of wind blew truck, Jack, drum, and Parker off the road almost into the bay before the wiry fishing captain could wrestle the steering wheel and get back on the pavement.

So he knew he had to nail up fast. He tore into the sandy yard beside his frame home on the beach at Islamorada, and he had boards nailed over the windows before supper. With things tied down, the twelve Parkers sat down and ate. One of their eleven children was married. The other ten were there in the lamplight, around the dinner table.

Everything that happened that night happened between eight and nine

49
▲

o'clock. In the next few days, Captain Parker was to find upward of thirty clocks stopped between those hours.

Death swept past Alligator Reef lighthouse first, five miles southeast of the beach home where the Parkers were having coffee.

Down on the lower platform of the lighthouse after supper, leaning on the rail and watching the wind pick up, was J. A. Duncan, one of the lighthouse keepers, a steady and reliable man. "I looked up," Duncan told the captain later, "and there was a wave coming at me that I fully believe was ninety feet high. I barely made it to grab hold of the ladder, when it broke over the light, and how I held on and why I wasn't drowned, I can't say. Then the wave went on, and the three of us in the lighthouse spent the rest of the night sitting on the stairs halfway up to the top of the light."

The great storm wave went on, sweeping down on the veterans and the administrators who had stopped playing poker hours before, when they began looking for the train. It roared on down on the Conch fishermen, and the Parker family around the dinner table. The first thing that happened there in the captain's house, was that the porch roof went off and huddled up against the house. He heard a most peculiar roar. He kicked a board off the window and stuck his head out on the lee side, and there was the rising ocean at the window sill.

They floated.

The roof went off. One wall was ripped away, leaving holes in the floor where the studs had been. An old iron bed got wedged into one of the holes. The captain and his wife put the little kids on the bed, and then he put a mattress over them so that they wouldn't be hurt by flying debris. One son was hurled against a window, and he put out his arm to save his face. The shattering glass cut the palm of the boy's hand off. He hung onto the bed along with his father and mother and the older children. The little fellows cried until they couldn't cry anymore.

First the wind was from the northeast, and since their beach at Islamorada faces almost south, they were washed into the ocean. There was the roar of the wind, a savage, brutal beast of a wind, louder than a locomotive right on top of you. Suddenly the wind slacked, failed, gasped fitfully. It was like a great animal dying, gasping for breath.

There were two minutes of that lull. "Daddy," said one child, "When I breathe I don't get any air! My lungs get no good of it!"

They were in the eye of the storm. The captain later found his barometer, stuck at 26.55. All they knew then was that if the lull had been drawn out to three minutes, they felt they would have strangled for want of air.

Over on Lignum Vitae Key, four miles away, Uncle Willard Sweeting came out into the calm in the hurricane's center. He got a half hour of dead calm. He stood outside and lighted matches that burned down to his finger tips. In that calm, Uncle Willard picked two veterans out of the water, who had floated over the bay from Camp Five, holding onto a telephone pole.

The Parker family floated in their wrecked home, in the fitful bit of the lull that was their portion. Now the night was not all black, but they wished it was. There had been some thunder and lightning before the storm broke, but none during the hurricane. Now, in the lull, there were balls of fire in the air. Suddenly they appeared, here and there, all around, gone in an instant.

"Daddy! A ball of fire big as a five-gallon can come at me! It scares me!"

The wind picked up, puff, puff, and then the shrieking fury was full upon them again from the southwest.

"Edney," said Mrs. Parker, "I can't hang on anymore!"

"Dammit, woman!" roared her husband above the wind, "You can't leave me alone with all these chillun! You hang on!"

And sometime that night about eleven o'clock, their weird vessel that had been a home washed ashore about a mile down the beach from where the terrible voyage began. And they were all still there, and all unhurt except the boy with the cut on his hand. The littlest one of the children, eleven months old, was asleep.

"Next day, all of us that were alive knew it took everything we had to make it through the night. And we very well knew that everything we had wouldn't have been enough it it hadn't been for the Lord's help," Captain Parker said.

But the days that followed in that week of horror, that was worse. Because the way help came from their fellowmen to the handful of battered survivors in the hard-hit Keys seemed so often a fumbling thing. And it was a very good thing that Captain Parker and his Conch neighbors had formed the habit of independence of the rest of Florida and the U.S.A.

The next morning they walked around in a world they hardly recognized. They found they were one of the very few families on Upper or Lower Matecumbe that didn't have someone killed or missing. Of the seventy-nine members of Captain John Russell's family, only eleven were alive. Nobody looked quite sane that Captain Parker saw. They seemed like they had been hit on the head. They found Alvin Pinder, Mrs. Parker's brother, wandering around in a daze, with nothing on but a little bit of a rag of an undershirt. He had bumps and lacerations, but he got alright.

And there at the railroad station that morning stood the train that was to take the veterans to the mainland and safety. The locomotive stood. The ten cars behind it were torn loose from the engine and flung on their sides off the track. An eternity ago, yesterday, Captain Parker had called for this train to take more than two hundred men living in tents to safety. Where were they now?

"Hey! Help!" came exhausted voices from a freight car lying on its side, with the open door down. He helped get Johnny Good and Anthony Thompson out of that car.

Good told him, "We got in the train about eight, and just afterward it got washed over, with the open door down. All night long we've been in there with some drums floating around and banging us. One time I could just keep my head above water."

In those cars, in all, were thirteen men from the Keys. "A wave of water fifteen or twenty feet high came in and knocked over all the cars," they said, "then it went on, and that was the end of the water, or we would all have been drowned for sure."

Later, when the train dispatcher cleared up, he told Captain Parker that the train stopped to take on water, and there it stayed when the wave hit it. "Good thing, too. If it had reached Camp Five, it would have been washed into the sea, for the railroad bed was washed away there, along with the camp." The train had left Miami at 4:25 they found.

Before the storm, one of the men had put some matches in a jar with a screw top and the jar in his pocket. They made a fire. They dried out some soggy bread that was lying about still in wrappers, and drank some warm Coca-Colas. It rained all day, except between three or four in the afternoon. Finally, there were about forty people huddled under a wall left standing at Rusty Gaines's place, that Tuesday after their world had been washed away.

They were lucky it rained, because all the cisterns that held the rainwater the Keys then drank had been blown away, and there was no way of getting fresh water except from the heavens. They got it in buckets.

For a while that seemed the only thing heaven was going to send them, for the sullen sea raged, and bridges were gone between the islands and the mainland. Finally, walking down the road in the rain came Dr. Grover C. Franklin, an old friend of Edney's from Coconut Grove, eighty miles north. He came in the first rescue party to land on Matecumbe, and he brought medical supplies.

"Doctor," said Captain Parker, "there are some people I want you to shoot with morphine."

"Take me to them, Edney," said the doctor.

Some of the men pushed an old truck, and it was a funny thing, they got it started. Dr. Franklin and the captain found a man at Camp Five sitting against a wall with a piece of two-by-four run through him. He was calm, peaceful, conscious. The two-by-four went in under his ribs and came out above his kidneys.

"I'll give you a shot of morphine before I pull this out," said Dr. Franklin.

The man said, "When you pull it out, I'm going to die. Don't give me a shot, Doc. Have you got a drink?"

"No," they had to tell him.

"Have you got a beer?" he said.

"Why, man, there's plenty of beer around here, but it's so hot you wouldn't want to drink it!" Parker told him.

"Give me a beer," the man said, and Parker got him a beer from the shambles of a bar, and he drank it.

"Give me another beer," he said, and he drank that. Then he said, "Pull it out, Doc."

Dr. Franklin pulled it out, and puff! the man died like a light goes out.

But on that rainy Tuesday, very few men from the other world showed up besides Dr. Franklin. The bridge was out at Snake Creek, and nobody could get across there for the currents raged through that gap between Plantation and Windley Key. And the dead and injured lay, mostly down a ten-mile stretch where the wind and rain had placed them Monday night.

Wednesday was worse. There was no more rain, and an iron hot sun came out on leafless islands. There were no leaves on any tree. The palms were gone. The hard mangroves died where they stood, leaves stripped, and the trunks were to be there a decade later, grey ghosts on that strip of coast.

Men in little boats from the mainland who landed along the beaches to help the survivors, fell to arguing who would be boss as soon as they hit the beach. There were nine bosses to every one worker.

The bodies among the mangroves swelled. They were the bodies of Captain Parker's friends and neighbors. By Wednesday it was getting hard to identify their features. Many of the volunteers were willing but weak, and they went back home after helping to get the first body out of the swamps. The National Guard was sent in. They couldn't do anything but police; they couldn't work.

The Red Cross, toward week's end, set up a relief office at Tavernier. But before they could do anything to help, they had to fill out forms and have them okayed by headquarters. And the forms came back saying, "You have made no permanent plan for rehabilitation."

Homes gone, stores gone, boats gone, lime groves and farms gone, families missing—the people who went to Tavernier for help from the Red Cross hardly had the strength to cuss when they were told they had to make a "permanent plan for rehabilitation."

Captain Parker wasn't going anywhere for help. He took command of a crew of Negroes sent down from Miami by FERA head Bill Green and began to pull the bodies of his friends and neighbors out of the mangroves. The sun blazed, and the bodies swelled, and the stench grew.

Wednesday, Miami very slowly came to about what was happening on the Keys, and the first of the injured reached the mainland. By week's end more than a hundred veterans were in beds that filled the halls of Miami's hospitals. Some of them had ducked bullets in the trenches in France, but they had nowhere to go when that wave came at them.

Jim Barker and Louis Allen came down from the Miami police department, and they worked in gas masks, identifying the dead that Captain Parker and his ever-changing crew were dragging out of the roots.

By the end of the week, Barker developed a new technique of fingerprinting. He put a rubber glove on his hand. He slipped the skin off the hand of a putrescent, unrecognizable corpse over the glove on his own hand. Then down he pressed on the ink pad, to get the fingerprints of men whose faces were gone.

"Funny," said Barker, "the fingertips last longer than any of the rest of the skin."

Of the 210 dead veterans finally identified, more than one hundred were named through this method. As fast as Barker took prints, he sent them to Miami. There the army had sent a fingerprint expert with army records of the men in the camps, and for days he sat in the balcony of a Miami hotel checking out the prints of the Keys' victims.

Somebody in alphabet officialdom ordered CCC boys down from Miami to collect the dead. Captain James Cain, USN, is still angry today because as Ensign Cain in the conservation camp, he had to send those teenage kids into that stench.

Not long after the National Guard landed, Captain Parker had a little trouble with one of their offiicers, a man named Carter. The captain went to what was left of his house to look for something. He was walking straight and talking soft, but the lines on his face had deepened to trenches.

The National Guard officer began talking around about martial law.

Parker didn't feel like talking that day. He looked through the guardsman, got what he wanted, and went on about his business, which was pulling out bodies.

In Miami, veterans from the Keys were being buried in a cemetery that held soldiers of the Spanish American War who had died with yellow fever.

Ernest Hemingway came up from Key West and helped pull bodies out of the mangrove and went back and flayed officialdom for the sick-sweet stench of rotting human flesh that hung over Matecumbe.

In Miami, Harry Hopkins sent Aubrey Williams to conduct for its WPA an investigation with a foregone conclusion. The conclusion was that any blame for not getting the veterans out would have to be spread around so generally, that no survivor of those men could sue the government.

Parker, straight and tough and brown and wrinkled, went on pulling dead men out of the swamp. At Camp Five, they found thirty-nine bodies of men stacked by the water in a heap like you stack cordwood.

The captain found his boat, too, back in the network of mangroves. A few weeks before he had given the boat a fresh coat of the best white yacht paint, at twelve dollars a quart. The paint was black, and he could take his hand and rub it off right down to the wood. He found the wall of his house, and on a nail hung the coffee bag with which his daughter had made Cuban coffee Monday night.

On Long Key somebody found a barometer stuck at 26.35 inches. When the accuracy had been verified, that reading became the record low for these times. The weathermen figured pressure gradients and finally said the wind probably blew 250 miles an hour between Matecumbe and Long Keys that night. Nobody believed them but Parker and the other people who lived through it.

Word came down Friday that all the dead were to be cremated henceforth. And the little fishing captain and his crew of corpse collectors piled high the ghastly pyres.

It was toward the end of the week when Edney found the bodies of Ed Albury's wife and child, and he told Philbrick, the funeral director, to send down metal caskets. He was helping Ed put his folks in the caskets when Carter, the National Guardsman came up.

"Orders are that all the dead are to be cremated!" barked the officer.

A hatchet lay at hand. Mangroves are so tough they dull any blade quickly, and Captain Parker had freshly sharpened that hatchet. Ed Albury picked it up, and started toward the guard officer, with the hatchet in his hand, and no emotion at all on his face.

"Maybe I should let you kill him, Ed," said Captain Parker, "but you got enough troubles." He pulled Albury away from the guard officer, and then he took out his pistol.

He pointed it at Carter, and his voice was very low and gentle and confiding with its Conch lilt. "If you give me any more trouble," said the leather-brown fishing captain to the guardsman, "I'm going to shoot you full of holes. I'm not going to report it to anybody. I'm burning eighty-two bodies at Islamorada this morning. I am in charge of the cremation. I will throw you on there and burn you, and nobody will know the difference."

And Captain Parker wondered if he shouldn't just go on and shoot the man.

Carter went off up to Tavernier, and complained to Doc Lowe, the justice of peace.

Doc told him, "Edney is a constable down there, and a constable has the same authority in his district that the sheriff has. I advise you to do like he says."

They didn't have any more trouble with the National Guard.

Today, the lean indomitable sixty-eight-year-old fishing captain rocks on his porch at Tavernier, looks out over the green water to the reef, and remembers that week like yesterday. When he remembers, his face is flooded with the happy look that comes to those who have had the manhood—and the luck—to live honorably through a savage rage of nature.

"I wouldn't give a million dollars for that night! But wouldn't go through it again for a million dollars!"

THE BEST WE COULD

I am an articulate artifact cast up by the tides of time from the primitive past of South Florida Social Work, a living relic of Dade County social work of the dawn era, when the only thing you really had to be able to do to be a case worker was to sign your name to a grocery order.

I want to tell you some stories about that primitive and often savage age, stories of comedy, stories of death. By listening to them you can see how far we have come, and feel good. But you may also see how far we have to go.

Before the hurricane of 1935, an ill wind that blew me out of social work and back into college, I had formed the opinion that social work is one of the world's noblest and most exciting professions. Nothing in my experience since then had changed my mind, except that today I feel it can be a far more vital calling in the next fifty years than it has been in the past half century—unless you are tempted to rest.

There is some evidence of that. You know the lines?

> *On the plains of hesitation, lie the bleaching bones of millions,*
> *Who at the dawn of victory lay down to rest, and resting, died.*

In taking a look at some highlights of the past, let us do it with a view to discovering what is applicable to now and pertinent to present problems. Let us draw away the blessed curtains of oblivion, and go back, then, to those days when Florida was known to social workers as a black state.

In 1921, The Miami Kiwanis Club decided they wanted to give baskets of groceries to the needy. That is the first "formal" welfare work I can discover in Miami. They invited Elizabeth Cooley, a field worker with the American Red

Cross, to come down and help them find somebody who needed help. Miami was launched on a land boom and dizzier than anything most of you have ever known. Miss Cooley and the Kiwanians went around together, but they could hardly find anybody who needed help.

But the Kiwanian impulse brought a star for your crown. You have heard Elizabeth Cooley King speak tonight. Jane Addams taught her, and she lived at Hull House. The person that resulted has made the whole state of Florida a better place to live.

By 1925, people had begun to lose their money. People were coming to Miami at the rate of six thousand a day, and leaving at the rate of two thousand a day. Many were stranded. Civic leaders organized a Community Chest. Isadore Cohen was secretary. The agencies allied in that first Chest drive were the American Children's Home; the Woman's Relief Association, which ran a day nursery; the Boy Scouts; the Girl Scouts; the Y.M.C.A. and the Y.W.C.A.

By 1926, people were standing in line at the Chest office, two hundred at a time, to be helped out of town. The boom had busted.

Miss Cooley resigned from the Red Cross in 1925 to take a job organizing a county welfare department for Palm Beach County on a district basis, with the help of county commissioners who were very interested in emergency aid to the transients who were stranded there. The Miami Community Chest soon lured her down here, and she came in July 1926 to set up a district welfare board. She had an office in the old Central School, one other social worker, and a typist. That made four social workers in Miami, with Miss Christian at the Red Cross and the medical social worker at Jackson Hospital. They all roomed together for many semesters.

The Community Chest raised money and created the Dade County Welfare Board to administer it. Hardly was the office arranged when one of the worst hurricanes ever to hit land swept squarely over Miami and Miami Beach.

The Welfare Board set up a commissary to feed people at Miami Avenue and Sixth Street. By January 1927 more than five thousand were on relief. The Salvation Army was wonderful. The First Baptist Church and the Monday Club and the Housekeepers Club did gallant volunteer work. In 1927, the Chest directors realized they couldn't raise nearly enough to assuage the suffering. They called in the county and the city officials and told them it looked like a long-term job. The county agreed to pay in three thousand a month, and the city $1,500 a month, and a board was set up representing the Chest, the

City, the County, Hialeah, Homestead, and South Miami.

In 1926, not long before the creation of this embryonic welfare setup, Miami had also given birth to another answer to crippled and starving people stranded here. That was the hobo express.

Police Captain Scarborough once explained: "All those beggars and crippled people on Flagler Street didn't look good when we were trying to make things nice for tourists. So I went to Judge Stoneman and asked if it would be alright for the police to round them up and send them back north where they came from. He said it would, and we did.

"Police would pick them up and put them on a freight train headed north. They would get out after they got into Broward County and fan out around the dairies, and kill cows to eat. So, pretty soon the Broward County officers would meet the express, and they would send them on to Palm Beach. Before the depression was over, the hobo express was running clear to Jacksonville. It didn't stop until civil rights came along, and they said it violated civil rights and we stopped."

It wasn't casework, but it was one answer.

The worst was yet to come. In 1928, another hurricane hit, devastating West Palm Beach and the Okeechobee region, where the smoke rose from the burning pyres of human bodies. It was not so bad in Miami, but it was bad enough.

The Chest didn't get its budget in 1928. They faced up to this in an interesting fashion. They told their social workers they would have to take a vacation without pay. Miss Cooley went to Hendersonville and ran a hotel that summer. And in 1929 the banks began to fail. Before that ended, they all closed except one. And old people sat on the curb and cried, and said, "What is this town going to do?"

The Community Chest sent Frank Pepper to Tallahassee to the legislature, and he got a bill passed in 1929, a population act for counties with over 100,000 people. It permitted Dade and Duval Counties to create a County Welfare Board.

The Dade County commissioners were perfectly furious. The governor sent down bonds to be signed to supply funds for welfare. The commissioners lost the bonds for a while.

Then County Commissioner Charlie Crandon told the Community Chest that the county didn't want any of that casework. They wanted somebody to go out and take groceries and come back and tend to her business. None of that sitting down and talking to people. The County Charities were created by the county government. The commission hired one worker—a gentle woman, a former home demonstration agent. She gave out what they called mother's pensions and emergency aid. Until she retired about 1956, her implied directive from the county commission was still basically "Don't let them faint in the streets from hunger."

The Community Chest continued to do what it could for the mounting tide of unemployed. George Estill, president of the Florida Power and Light, gave them old light poles. They set up a wood yard where they sent men to chop wood, and they paid them. They had old clothes sales.

Mostly, things were getting blacker. But in 1929, one wonderful thing happened. Florida social workers had gotten together and created a State Conference of Social Work. President in 1929 was—Miss Cooley. Florida was one of four black states, with no workman's compensation. All a worker injured on the job could do was sue. Social workers had seen so often what followed: "Old ambulance-chasing lawyers got it all, and there was nothing left for the man who was hurt."

So, in 1929, the State Conference of Social Work decided to lobby for passage of the State Workman's Compensation Bill. They raised money and hired Mrs. Gertrude Fuller, an eloquent orator out of Chautauqua. She went into every one of the sixty-seven counties of Florida and dug up dozens of cases of injuredworkers in each county. They made a file. They took it to the legislature. Mrs. Fuller spoke on the floor of the legislature. They lost, by one vote, and they were sick, but they didn't stop. They plugged away for years. They got labor unions to help. When the New Deal came along they got Secretary of Labor Frances Perkins to help. She wrote to Governor Dave Sholtz. President Roosevelt came to Florida. He talked to Sholtz in Jacksonville, and one of the things they talked about was workman's compensation.

Finally, in the 1935 session, Sholtz told the legislature the bill was a must, and it passed. Miss Cooley had chaired the lobbying committee of the social workers over those years, and that will be a nice thing on her passport to heaven.

The Community Chest Welfare Board folded at the bottom of the depression, in 1932.

Since 1928, Miami Beach had had a branch office of the board in City Hall. T. J. Pancoast asked Miss Cooley to organize a Miami Beach City Welfare Department. She took the job at thirty-five dollars a week.

Of the result of that work, now being carried on so competently by Barbara

Jack, the Dade County Family and Child Care Survey commented last year:

> The Social Service Department of Miami Beach since 1928 has
> provided an outstanding welfare program adapted to a community
> with a high ratio of older persons in its population. Today, this city
> offers modern flexible casework services to local residents, which
> make up for deficiencies in State and County programs. The
> program is sensitive to people's needs and is a model of what might
> be provided by the State and County if their programs were fully
> effective. Despite this long period of development, the Department
> is still not specially sanctioned by provisions of the City Charter.

If the Beach has been backward about admitting publicly and officially that it has a welfare problem and a welfare program, it has not been backward about raising money for it. Over there in the thirties they would raise five thousand dollars in one night in a benefit at Flamingo Park. They had a good board, and City Manager Claude Renshaw protected the department as best it may be done from the election-time assaults of some city councilmen.

(If you think you've been hearing a lot about Elizabeth Cooley, let me tell you something else. When she resigned, over the protests of Mr. Renshaw, at the age of seventy-three in 1956, she went back to school to get her master's degree in social work—and this fascinates the hell out of me. I wish the same to you.)

But let us turn from the social work excellencies of that Miami Beach, at which all of our New England-type intellectuals sneer, and look at Miami in 1932.

Miami went off in another direction. They hired the first truant officer in this town to head their city welfare department. She resembled the Queen of Hearts in *Alice's Adventures in Wonderland* in looks and in temperament. Neither her clients nor her colleagues would have been surprised to hear her holler, "Off with his head!" She had an interesting compulsion. She would not pay out one cent of city welfare money for food after the FERA came to town. But she would readily pay for transportation to send people back to where they came from. She would persuade   former Michigan dwellers that they were residents of Detroit, even though they had lived in Miami for ten years, and give them fare to go back "home."

The Florida State Welfare Board was created in 1932, with Marcus Fagg as its first head. This board and the act creating it provided some funds, a trickle of assistance, in the form of a certain kind of aid for children.

61
▲

It was the bottom of the depression, and along came the alphabet agencies. Toward the end of Hoover's time there was PWA, and then, with Roosevelt, FERA and WPA.

These letters are like brands on my heart, representing as they do to me both the pain and the challenge of social work.

I was twenty-one, and I wanted to go to Key West. Key West, once the richest city per capita on the Atlantic seaboard, was then the poorest. The sponge fishermen, and the cigar makers, and the U.S. Navy had moved out. They left behind people who would rather starve than live anywhere else than Key West. They said, "The Navy will come back. Let the government support us until it does."

When state FERA administrator Julius Stone discovered the nature of the Key West Conch, he dropped plans for transferring population and launched a project to recreate the dying city. Everybody in the Key West city administration was on relief. To be mayor was a relief job. I heard they were hiring social workers at twenty-five dollars a week.

So I checked with a friend, Ellen Knight, another social worker who is a star in the crown of your profession, and is now Ellen Knight Whiteside. She said, "You don't want to go to Key West." I do, still. But she convinced me I would rather be something called a caseworker in the Miami office of the FERA at fifteen dollars a week. I quit the *Miami News* —where I was writing obituaries, food and fashions—and became a caseworker.

FERA was purely federal. The spirit behind it was Harry Hopkins, a one-time Red Cross social worker who had sold Roosevelt on social work in New York State. The setup he organized for federal emergency relief had a wonderful theoretical decency in its claims for individual consideration of individual problems casework. These claims both greatly advanced and crippled social work. It postulated that there would not be a rubber-stamp dole. But because there were so few qualified social workers in existence, it allowed people like me at twenty-one to call themselves social workers. And lots worse.

We did the best we could, but a generation hates the name of "social work," largely because of us. Some were sadists, some were sentimentalists, some were bureaucrats—and these last were the worst. The emotions that activate sadists and sentimentalists ebb and flow. But the dead, total lack of emotion that infects a bureaucrat is with us always, and it is one of the great threats of our lifetime.

The philosophy behind FERA is still something that thrills me. The actual, fatuous day-by-day working of the thing was something that still gives me the triple vomits. I got the district on North Miami Avenue, from Fifth to Thirteenth Street. My clients were mostly unemployed Cuban cigar makers and aging prostitutes. Their problem was hunger.

The Cubans had to face the fact that the cigar industry had migrated to Tampa. The prostitutes faced the fact that their youth had migrated—further than Tampa.

Florida was, again, a black state. Florida could not match federal funds for starving people with one red cent, they told Washington, and maybe they were right. We had had a premature and long depression. The FERA, with nothing but federal funds, provided two forms of relief for certified clients the workers had investigated. The clients got work cards which gave them three days of work at $2.60 a day. While the Republicans beefed about lazy men raking leaves, my clients were showing me muck sores on their legs from digging ditches in the mangrove swamps around Matheson Hammock, the first Dade County mosquito control.

There were jobs for women, too. They sewed. One project was making blue curtains for FERA administrator Julius Stone's yacht. He was Jim Farley's law partner. Mrs. Stone had blue eyes.

In a week when they didn't get a work card, they might get a grocery order from me, maximum, two dollars. My allocation for direct relief for the eighty families in my district was often as low as two hundred dollars a month. In addition to this fatuous federal welfare, clients might get sheets from the Red Cross, food from the Salvation Army, and handouts from the county farm where prisoners raised vegetables. As to medical help, I will never forget the county welfare head telling me of a pregnant woman in labor I was trying to get into Kendall Hospital, "After all, Miss Wood, they's been born in a manger."

Those were the resources when I was in social work.

Nevertheless, I might still be there were it not for the hurricane of 1935. On the Florida Keys, social worker Harry Hopkins had conceived a brilliant solution to the problem of the veterans who kept marching on Washington and making trouble. Herbert Hoover sent out MacArthur, on a white horse, to charge these men. But Harry Hopkins and Franklin D. Roosevelt sent them to Matecumbe Key to build a highway to Key West. In about two years they built almost two hundred feet of causeway. You had to be a veteran and go to Washington and make trouble to get into one of these camps. They got thirty dollars a month, cots in tents, food, and plenty of time for fishing. The food was wonderful. Steaks and crawfish with drawn butter, and ice cream for lunch and dinner. The word was, "Keep them happy and keep them out of Washington."

I was sent down as a private in a task force of social workers to interview the veterans, so that the camps could be liquidated on a casework basis. Two days after we finished our interviews, the worst hurricane ever to hit land anywhere liquidated them.

The bureaucrats passed the buck and the veterans died. More would have died had it not been payday, Labor Day weekend, when so many were in Miami. Their rotting bodies were burned, and the stench drove me out of bureaucracy—because I knew that if I had been responsible, I might have been one of the ones who played it safe and passed the buck and caused it all.

The days and weeks that followed that hurricane were a disgrace to Miami and south Florida. Neighbor failed neighbor; organized relief failed. Only the people of Homestead, led by Mayor Preston Bird, did gallant relief work. The head of the Red Cross here had a nervous breakdown as a result, and could not get going again for a year. I suppose I was lucky that wind only blew me back to college.

But while I was going through this catharsis of death and disgust, something wonderful was happening for Florida in Tallahassee in 1935. The 1935 State Welfare Act, providing categorical assistance, was passed. Conrad Van Hyning wrote it. He is another star in your crown, and a lovely man. Harry Hopkins sent him down here in the FERA. He was a professional social worker, a former assistant district welfare commissioner in Washington, and a close friend and valued ally of Hopkins. It might have been possible to get Van Hyning to head your present county welfare department had Metro County Manager Hump Campbell known or cared anything about social work.

Van Hyning made this the first state in the country to set up welfare by districts. The virtue of that, of course, is that areas were large enough to allow staffing by qualified social workers. To do his job, he had to sell the Welfare Act to sixty-seven boards of county commissioners, for in its initial years it was supported by county funds. It is interesting to note that the wool hat boys in north Florida were most receptive and put it over. They only feared welfare as all southerners do, because anything adequate to keep a person alive might take Negroes out of the fields. Dade County, then as now, had both that fear, and the other fear, the resort fear. Dade was afraid that subsistence aid would attract snowbirds who would live off relief in the sunshine.

And who did they get to staff the district welfare office in 1937? Why, Elizabeth Cooley! There were never enough to go around! She organized the

District Welfare Board. Back to the Beach she went a year later, when one of Governor Fred Cone's district board appointees demanded from her a list of names of welfare recipients so that he could demand from them their votes.

Highlight of social work in the 1940s, as I remember it, was a study of state institutions made in 1945 by my old friend, Ellen Knight Whiteside. Ellen grew up, went to New York School of Social Work, stopped laughing at politicians, and learned how to cope with them. Governor Millard Caldwell created for her a job called Assistant to the Governor on State Institutions. She went and took a long look at the Florida Farm Colony (for the feeble-minded), Chattahoochee (for the crazy) and the Crippled Children's Commission.

Nothing was the matter with the Crippled Children's Commission except they harbored the idea that they had a fifty-thousand-dollar fund that didn't exist, and they couldn't pay their hospital bills. A deficiency appropriation bill cured this.

But at the Florida Farm Colony, Ellen found something that parallelled Nazi concentration camps. The old doctor who ran it was even outspoken in favor of mercy killings. The gentle mongoloids, the little gay peanut-headed microcephalics, and the docile idiots and morons were living in dank, dark, boarded, crowded rooms, in conditions of incredible filth. When I read Ellen's reports in newspapers I shuddered, because if there is a hereafter I may have to answer for those conditions as a Florida citizen. Chattahoochee was worse.

Ellen educated newspapermen and legislators, fast and eloquently. She did a beautiful job of starting a cleanup, in the tradition of social work. One result is that the new Sunland Training Center near Ft. Myers, that opened this month, is lavishly equipped and beautiful. The only thing you think now is that if the people who are committed there are smart enough to use some of those school and therapy facilities, they shouldn't be there. The world is being run by people no smarter.

But let me summarize what I think from this look at the primitive past of social work.

As the world fills up, it is getting lonelier. People get into a variety of trouble, far from families and old friends, and must more and more turn for help to strangers. Welfare agencies give the help of strangers, and social case-work is the best way ever developed to do this.

Social work is a double job in daily practice. You must represent organized society, as a member of your agency, to your clients. Like it or no, it is a role forced on you because that is the way your clients see you. You must also represent your clients to organized society. You must help them to find a way through the labyrinthine ways and the red tape of existence today as an individual ally.

We have also, however, a third duty, in which we have tended to fail, with a few notable exceptions, as my history has perhaps indicated.

You must not only represent organized society, you must fight to change it when it is stupid, inadequate, and cruel. Too many have ducked the responsibilities of trying to change black situations and make them at least gray.

Florida is still the lowest state in the nation in aid to dependent children.

Casework, you know, can't effect the great changes in welfare that makes thousands of lives happier or more endurable. Those changes require politics, lobbying, publicity, propaganda, and a dedicated fight to bring them about.

Some of my best friends are social workers, too. But you do tend to be somewhat "beat." The beatnik is nothing new, but he is the greatest threat to democracy today. Today he is called "beat," and a "white negro," though the courage and drive of black Negroes is now making this inappropriate. Over the ages he has also been known as a skeptic, a stoic, a cynic, and a nihilist. The beat attitude has always had a thrilling appeal for intellectuals. Nobody ever phrased the beat attitudes more persuasively than Housman: "Be still my heart, be still, the arms you bear are brittle. Earth and high heaven are fixed of old and fashioned strong." There is a terrible danger in the appeal of those lines.

Perhaps the beat philosophy does not seem to you to have made much headway in the United States, but that its exponents are simply young men with beards who don't smile and cultivate indifference. But the beat men engulfed Europe forty years ago, and their indifference and loneliness made possible the totalitarian states.

Indifference is democracy's greatest threat. Democracy is a slow, tedious, clumsy thing of compromises. Like Winston Churchill, I believe it is the worst form of government, except for every other one I know. It is too easy to sneer at politicians and newspaper writers, who shape democracy. It is much harder for you to educate these men and women who have such a major effect on our lives. Some have stood up to this responsibility brilliantly. Most duck it.

But when we do rise to this responsibility, I do believe with all my heart, that we have proved that a good social worker is but little lower than the angels.

CORAL GABLES

A massive man who could sell because he was sold, convince because he was convinced, built Coral Gables. He was George Merrick.

They are celebrating the twenty-fifth anniversary of the town starting today, and they are saying that any history of the place is the history of George Merrick.

They think he did a good job.

He was unique in an era that produced some great and gaudy figures. He built a town that has a special character.

Merrick and his city had great good luck in capturing the outstanding virtues and avoiding the outstanding vices of the wildest era this area has ever known—the Great Land Boom of the 1920s.

In the quarter of a century since the town was chartered, a generation has grown up out there that calls the town home. They have that in common with Merrick, for it was home to him.

He planted snap beans in the glade that was to become the Coral Gables Country Club golf course.

Old Spanish tile aged to dark browns and reds, faded pink stucco, and hand-faced coral rock meant home to a generation that wasn't born when the Gables city charter was granted on April 8, 1925.

The same thing meant "home" to young Merrick.

Perhaps because he was dealing with land and trees and scenes he knew and deeply loved, Merrick and his Coral Gables held themselves to an integrity of design and detail that was remarkable for a dizzy period in local building and planning.

When Henry Flagler was consulted on the laying out of Miami's streets in the 1890s, he took a dim view and insisted that streets thirty feet wide were plenty wide. Not so George Merrick twenty-five years later with his town.

Fifty-, seventy-five- and one-hundred-foot boulevards keep that suburb from being niggardly. No traffic jams there except for very momentary ones when everybody from Tropical Park racetrack tries to go home down Bird Road at once.

George Merrick was no binder boy and no cynic. He wasn't down here to make his pile and run when the boom collapsed. He made his money in Coral Gables and he lost it there. He lived to see his town come back to a solid financial footing. He came back himself. The town and the man ran along parallel lines in spirit and fortune for as long as he lived.

To thousands of young men and women today, Coral Gables is as dear and familiar as a vastly different Coral Gables was to young George Merrick forty years ago. He took the name of his town from the name of his family's home on Coral Way.

Men and women who've grown up there describe it something like this: "It's a clean, green, leisurely town. There are no slums; no dirt is swept under the rugs. Policemen and bus drivers in Coral Gables are your friends. Lawns are wider and greener than anywhere else in, maybe, the world."

Miami Beach has far more wealth and fame. The Gables doesn't mind; it is a town of home folks.

Gables residents, say her critics, are slackers: They make their money in the great world of Miami and retreat to their own little snug haven every night, leaving said Miami minus their tax money to solve its cruel problems.

Gables folks, her critics continue, are typical nice suburbanites. They keep their own little corner clean and ignore the poverty, vice, crime, slums, and sundry other woes of the rest of Dade County.

"In this imperfect world," sigh the Gables folks, "it is something important to keep one little corner clean."

And to say to anybody who has grown to voting age in Coral Gables that it is just a "money town" is to make his hackles rise. In the thirties, chances are, he and his neighbors were as broke as his hometown.

A high percentage of people who lived in this suburb in the thirties knew worry about rent, mortgages, and all the rest of the expenses of living. One reason they still live in the Gables now is that it is a pleasant town to be broke in, too. More pleasant than most, they say.

For once, the chamber of commerce of a town agrees with its old-timers.

Says the Chamber of Commerce: "Coral Gables, its design, its past, and future are Merrick."

He was that rarest bird of south Florida's early days—a pioneer. Just coming first doesn't make a pioneer. An awful lot of first comers in this area were promoters—they came to exploit, to get their bag of gold, and to go back north.

Merrick's father didn't come here for that. He came here to homestead, to plant, to live in and be a part of the country.

His daddy was a congregational minister, Solomon Greasley Merrick, and his mother was Althea Fink Merrick. George was born at Springdale, Pennsylvania, on June 3, 1886, but his moving around began when he was a year old and his father became pastor of a church in Gaines, New York.

The old Pilgrim Church in Duxbury, Massachusetts. called his father when George was eight, and there he went to Partridge Academy for a year before the family moved to Florida in 1898.

The Reverend Mr. Merrick was one of the early discoverers of the idea that it is stupid to be cold. Because of poor health, he decided to move his wife and seven children to a homestead near Miami in 1898.

It was a terrible winter in Duxbury, Massachusetts. He lost one of his little twin daughters with croup. He decided he would move somewhere under the sun and give up the ministry and make a living from the land. His forebears had been Scots who first settled on the western shore of Maryland, but the ministry had meant a wandering life to him and his family. So he looked in the directory of congregational ministers and wrote the Reverend James Bolton in Coconut Grove to ask him about farmland he might acquire.

One Harry Gregory had just proved a one-hundred-acre homestead, about four miles from Coconut Grove, Mr. Bolton replied, and he could buy it from him for $1,100. Mr. Merrick sent the money down and in 1898 came south to his land with his oldest son, thirteen-year-old George.

When he saw it, he would have turned around and gone home, but George insisted that they stay. It was pine- and palmetto-covered rock crossed by a finger glade too low for trees.

Then Coral Way was a wagon track hacked through tall pines; panthers followed the meat-loaded wagons down this track. The Granada golf course was a lake each fall and a bean field in winter.

When the Merrick children first came to Miami, it was a rough-and-ready town where you went to get your haircut, but otherwise might avoid.

The family homesteaded 160 acres in the high pineland southwest of

Miami, built a shack, and then built a home of coral rock with a gabled roof that they later named Coral Gables.

They began to dynamite and plant grapefuit trees. Grapefruit were an exotic novelty to the country and brought fourteen dollars a bushel.

George cleared pineland and coral rocks, helped plant citrus and vegetables, and peddled them to the few hundred residents of Miami and to the Royal Palm Hotel.

In 1900 they brought Mrs. Merrick and the other four children down. The other children were Ethel, Medie, Helen and Charles. One more was to be born the following year, the first white child to be born in Coral Gables— Richard.

The years before the grove began to bear were the tough ones. George later wrote a poem about them. Ethel remembers one bitter night when the family all sat around the wood stove in the kitchen and shivered. Her father came in after a trip outside to look at the thermometer.

"If the wind doesn't begin to change to northeast in half an hour, we'll be ruined."

Ethel went in and knelt by the bed and prayed: "God, if you will change the wind to northeast or east, I'll be a good girl all my life!" she promised silently.

Half an hour later her father came in glowing. "The wind's changing toward the east. There'll be no frost."

It was a very tough country for an intellectual man and woman whose palms were not used to calluses. The little two-room frame house was unceiled when his family came down. Mrs. Merrick sewed unbleached muslin together in a great tent to line the walls and ceilings, because the snakes and the rats adventuring across the rafters made her nervous.

With this kind of start, it was a tremendous thing for Mr. Merrick to be able, by 1905, to have Williams De Gazell build him a great stone house with a wide porch all around. He was so proud of that house.

That house gave its name first to Coral Gables Plantation and then to the city itself.

Mrs. Merrick, who was a painter, drew the plans. It was fortunate they had lived in south Florida long enough to let the climate dictate the plan. It has a deep porch east, south and west to protect the windows from driving rain, and for sitting in the breeze. It has high ceilings. It has fireplaces. It is built four feet above the ground because they knew about fall floods.

Other settlers came in, whose names are now remembered in roads. Walter

Ludlum was an overseer for Mr. Merrick. Charles LeJeune was a member of the French nobility who left his native land because of duel trouble. He bought a grove on the road that bears his name, near the north campus of the University of Miami. The Merrick children's uncle, Worth St. Clair, who married Mrs. Merrick's sister, came down about 1903.

Grandpa Fink, Mrs. Merrick's father, came visiting. He had made a fortune in Fink's Magic Oil, an inherited family buiness. He bought a parcel of land opposite where the Miami post office now stands. They were offered $250,000 for the parcel in the boom. Mrs. Merrick got $2,500 out of the property in the depression, when Grandma Fink died.

During those years, after the grove began to bear, Mr. Merrick sold the fruit on the trees at a good price. The Coconut Grove Congregational Church asked him to be their minister, and he was for six years until his health failed. When he died he had made something.

As the oldest son, George transacted the business of the growing plantation until he entered Rollins College in 1907.

George was a big, hard-working boy. When he had a toothache or an earache, he would go out and throw rocks against the side of the barn, as hard as he could throw. He was the only Dade subdivider who, when the streets of his city came to a fruit tree, would have the fruit tree carefully dug up and set out again in a nearby lot.

He wrote poetry, and he wanted to make writing his life.

At Rollins he wrote, went in for oratory, and made a friend of Jack Baldwin, a fellow student who later helped him obtain financing for the real estate development of Coral Gables, and who also became one of the first city commissioners of the town.

Because his father wanted him to, he studied law at Rollins, and later for a year at New York Law School, then part of Columbia University. But when his father suddenly died, he came home in 1911 to manage the family business. For nine years he worked at building up the largest and most successful fruit and vegetable plantation in this end of the state, and at one time had a thousand acres planted.

The Merricks shipped the first carload of citrus out of Dade. In 1921, the last year before the city was born, they shipped ninety carloads of citrus.

Merrick's marriage to Eunice Peacock brought him a daughter of a pioneer for a wife. Her father, who came from England in 1878, was one of the founders of Coconut Grove and owner of the old Peacock Inn there.

Though to the rest of the country south Florida's boom of the twenties seemed to happen overnight, the man who lived here knew better. Merrick served an apprenticeship for a decade in real estate development before the wave of his fortune crested with the creation of Coral Gables in 1925.

"For, in ten years, " he said in an interview in 1925, the year of his greatest financial glory, "I worked night and day to build up a nucleus for the Coral Gables which consistently grew in my dreams. I never told anyone my plans, but as my profits in real estate grew, I bought adjoining land. The 160 acres the family originally owned increased to 300, then to 500, to 1,000, and finally to 1,600."

When the boom came, all of the Merrick children signed over their interest to George.

Denman Fink, Merrick's uncle who is now a professor of art at the University of Miami, helped the young man lay out his town in 1921. All the winding streets that were later to drive strangers mildly crazy were drawn on paper before any lots were sold.

It isn't myth that for two years Merrick sent his architects to the Mediterranean area and the South Seas to study designs which he believed were the best ones adaptable to south Florida.

None of them stayed sober but his uncle, Denman Fink.

(Yea, friend, those were the days, when a onetime candidate for the United States presidency, William Jennings Bryan, was hired at a rumored salary of $50,000 a year to make daily speeches at the Venetian pool!)

The late Phineas Paise, A.I.A., was supervising architect, and Frank Button was landscape architect. With Professor Fink, they produced the mixed Spanish and Italian design which Merrick chose to call Mediterranean. (Old Gables residents pray only that present building styles age as pleasantly.) Merrick had a hope chest of $500,000 when he began his great venture in 1921, and that ran out in short order. It was then that he again met Baldwin, his Rollins classmate, who helped him get financing from an insurance company to build the first one hundred homes in his town.

In the fabulous year of 1925 he pledged $5,000,000 to a University of Miami, to be located on 160 acres he donated. He wasn't promoting them, and he didn't mean it as a gesture, though that it proved. In 1924 the cornerstone of the Coral Gables Congregational Church was laid, and today it is considered one of the finest mission-type churches in the country. St. Joseph's Academy came in that year. It is now the Church of the Little Flower, led since its beginning by the Reverend Father Thomas Comber. In those early years Colonel J. R. Williams directed the Coral Gables Military Academy, and that building now houses the Merrick Demonstration School.

Merrick compassed the usual history of several generations in his own life-time when he became one of the town's first commissioners on April 29, 1925. In that month the Coral Gables corporation was formed, and the City of Coral Gables was incorporated with the first city commission composed principally of corporation officers named by the state. (It was to be the principal ammu-nition in a somewhat bitter recall election three years later that these offi-cers were not elected.)

Commissioners besides Merrick were: Telfair Knight, corporation vice-president and general manager; Baldwin, corporation treasurer, and F. Wingfield Webster, chairman of the corporation's executive committee. E. E. "Doc" Dammers—he was a medicine show doctor and sold lots from a mule-drawn cart—was first mayor of the city.

Sure, they were giddy days. In little more than five years, $150,000,000 worth of building was done in Coral Gables. Jan Garber's and Paul Whiteman's orchestras were brought down to sell lots. A million dollars was spent in 1925 on advertising alone. Three thousand salesmen were working. Gondolas and their native gondoliers were imported. The $10,000,000 Miami Biltmore Hotel with its swimming pool and 18-hole golf course was formally opened on January 15, 1926.

Then it was all gone, completely gone. And the Merrick children all loved their oldest brother quite as much as they always had, which was quite a lot. His mother sold off lots in Block 10 for four hundred dollars each to live on in the depression, and then she and Ethel began to take in roomers and called the home Merrick Manor.

After George lost everything in the bust he drank a lot. Once in the late 1920s he decided to dry out and give up booze. He sailed over to Key Biscayne, then a lonely island, and stayed a few days. After walking down the beach one evening he lay down on the sand to take a nap. When he turned over and stretched out his arm, he touched what turned out to be a full bottle of booze, washed in from a rumrunner. Chug-a-lug. Some years later he did dry out, and was appointed U.S. Postmaster for Miami.

The city he loved and did such a good job on will keep his place in history.

73

Xanadu

Make a trip of discovery among the blue springs of the Suwanee River country and you will wonder (whisper it!) why anyone ever comes on through to south Florida.

These springs make that land perfect for playing hooky.

Sprinkled all across north Florida are hundreds of the superlative natural swimming holes. Funnel shaped, they shade from crystal water on the sandy shore, to sky blue, then to the deepest royal blue at the center. The colors of these pellucid waters are clear as a bugle call.

You can float over the shafts where the cool water wells and see specks of mica glinting on sandy floors of caves, forty, sixty, ninety feet below, as though you looked through air. You can see the expression in the eyes of the bream, the curl in whiskers of the catfish, count mullet scales. The water from the spring streams away through the woods to the nearby river.

The splendid natural fountains are from twenty to two hundred feet wide. All the rains that fall in the porous limestone country go instantly underground to feed them.

Always a great green curtain of cypress, live oak, magnolia, hickory, and grape vines rim the water. The carpenter you hear in the woods, rapping with a jack hammer, is a pileated woodpecker.

You drive in and agree with the country woman that the water is "cold enough to make ice tea out of."

You come out light, with years washed off you, and the hot summer sun of Florida is benign on your back.

A handful of the springs are, of course, famous, exploited, commercialized, and heavily advertised. Every one deserves the praise of the most lavish ad writer, but the hundreds of others hidden in the woods are more exciting to discover, for everybody that finds them feels Nature is hostess.

How do you find them? Go to almost any town between Gainesville and Tallahassee and ask. Ask, for example, at High Springs, and they will tell you how to wind four miles southeast to their Blue Springs, and three miles north to Hornsby Springs. Ask at Ft. White for the way to Ichtucknee Springs and The Jug. Ask at Branford for directions to Troy Springs where a Civil War cotton-carrying ship was scuttled to escape the Yankees and can be seen on the bottom by the west bank of the Suwanee.

Try along the Sante Fe River; scores of perfect springs feed it. Where it joins the Suwannee there are a dozen. Blue Springs east of Madison on State Road 6 is marked on road maps. July Springs, Darby Spring, Jenning's Spring, Nude Sink, Bug Spring, Fannin's Spring—their names are legion and they all mean beauty.

Gilchrist, Suwannee, Alachua, Lafayette, Marion, and Levy Counties all have a goodly share, for they are the counties of limestone that dissolves away in funnels, sinks, and fluted columns to allow the filtered water to boil up from underground caverns and rivers.

At the springs you meet farmers launching their boats to catch "little ole brim." Many of the swimmers bring their soap and the suds boil away instantly down the stream. If you feel young you can swing out on the rope that is always tied to an oak limb over the water, and drop in the heart of the spring. Professorial zoologists and geologists dive with face mask and flippers for blind crayfish and mastodon teeth.

The youngsters of the diving clubs of Ocala, Gainesville, and Tallahassee come with aqualungs and double tanks to explore the many chambered caves and corkscrew tunnels. Bob Brown of Lake City dived eighty feet to the bottom of Troy Springs on one gulp of air in his own lungs, without diving apparatus.

Everybody that ever finds a blue spring loves it, remembers, and returns. Too few vacationers know them. No signs point the way: you have to ask. You can camp in the blue springs country or you can room in a town and make exploring jaunts by car or boat. "No Trespassing" signs are almost unknown in the Suwannee country.

These blue and welling waters rimmed by southern forests should be memorialized, you may find yourself thinking, in imperishable poetry.

They have been.

Coleridge was reading William Bartram's book of travels in Florida, reading a description of the springs of Alachua. He fell asleep and woke up with the lines of "Kubla Khan" ready to write in his mind.

He paraphrased Bartram's description when he described,

> *Where Alph, the sacred river ran,*
> *through caverns measureless to man.*
> *Down to a sunless sea.*

So the blue springs filtered through the sleep of a peerless poet across an ocean.

You may make no poetry, catch no fish, but a day, a week, a time of playing hooky by the springs of the Suwanee River country will be a blue jewel in your memory for as long as you remember beauty.

TIMBER

Florida's last frontier, an awesome combination of wildest nature and newest machines, is a lumber camp in the Everglades.

We rode beside a man who has one of the world's most thoroughly damnable jobs. His name is Paul Miller, and he rides a caterpillar tractor that pulls the great cypress logs from the swamp where they are cut.

Up the logging road we came, with four logs dragging on steel cables behind the little "cat." That road was a narrow, winding stream of black, oily, stinking mud. We had to hold on with both hands, tight. The cat got hung up on rocks submerged in the river of ooze. Roots tangled and stalled it. The machine bucked and climbed at crazy angles. Twice we were convinced it was going to turn on over and bury us in that mud. And when we got in the clear for a moment and put on a little speed, the mud spattered up on us from the treads. The mud in that road made it look and smell like one long, twisting pig sty.

But the worst thing about Miller's job was not the pounding of the cat he drove, or the mud. It was the flies—yellow-striped deer flies, bigger than a house fly, smaller than a horse fly. They buzzed before our eyes and nose. When we opened our mouths they flew in. Everywhere they bit, they bit hard. Insect dope doesn't faze them.

It takes Paul Miller and his cat twenty minutes to haul some thousand feet of log the half mile out of the swamp to high ground. For any of you boys who are interested in making round trips into Hades eight times a day, the pay is eighty-five cents an hour, plus a house to live in.

We decided we would rather be treed by a panther than surrounded by those flies, and we talked to a man who had been treed by a panther.

Nathaniel Johnson, a Negro half-track driver, went out into the swamp looking for one of the logging crews, and got lost for eighteen hours. The boss of the camp, R. T. Goodson, sent out a searching party for Johnson, but they couldn't find him.

Along about dusk, Johnson said, he realized something was trailing him, and he shinnied up a pine tree. He looked down after he got a ways up, and saw the panther. The panther stayed at the bottom of the tree until dawn, and then he went away, and Johnson came down.

"No, sir, I wasn't particularly scared," Johnson said. "Panthers can climb, sure enough, but they won't usually go up a pine tree after you. I knew he'd go away when it got light. And I knew I'd get out alright."

Later we saw the skin of such a panther, big as that of a half-grown calf, with claws an inch long. This is the biggest cat that's ever been found by men in the United States.

Men on this job have seen deer in numbers. Three or four rattlesnakes are killed a week. There are cottonmouths in the swamps. Nobody worries much about the snakes. They are there, but not in the writhing abundance pictured by the more fervid imagination. They can be avoided. Men who are terrified of the thought of snakes just don't go into the Everglades to live and work.

This cypress cutting is being done south of the Tamiami Trail some sixty miles west of Miami by Cummer and Sons of Lacoochee. The camp where part of the workers live is a collection of neat, solidly-built cypress cabins four miles beyond Monroe Station, on the Trail. Four miles west of the camp is the little logging road that is bringing so much tribulation to men and machinery.

For two miles, as this road winds south through open stretches of the 'Glades to the stand of big cypress, it is dusty, bumping torture. Pitted bedrock comes to the surface, and a thin layer of gray marl that tops it here and there seems to be fast blowing away in swirls and clouds of dust. Then the road dips into the swamp, a dense hammock, where you meet mud and flies, and the torture is intensified.

We walked that last half mile into the swamp to meet the caterpillar tractor and ride out on it. It was a strange, fascinating walk, and could have even been wonderful, but for the flies. Only the logging road itself was muddy, where the tractors had bitten deep and churned up the underlying ooze. The ground alongside the track was soft and springy. The trees are one of the glories of this world. Along the logging track only the stumps of the big cypress remain, but there are plenty of smaller cypress, with their feathery spring-green tops. Slender Everglades palm thrust their heads sixty feet up into the sunshine. We saw many aromatic sweet gums, and several enormous black gum trees. Under the trees, covering the springy humus, were brilliant green ferns.

One bit of advice—if you go walking through that swamp, don't try any shortcuts. We went down the wrong turn, came to the end of the logging track, and found it had been abandoned. So we cut through an old burn, where the walking was easy, to another track to the east. For a minute or two we were lost. All of a sudden, we were sweating hard, and the flies were twice as thick, and the crows were cawing with a raucous jeer.

Then near at hand, a tractor roared as its motor was started, and we came to the sawing.

Negroes do the felling in there, two men to a saw. The moment one of those big trees began to go was bad. We felt guilty that our love for the look and the feel and the smell and all the wonderful enduring quality of cypress boards meant the death of one of those magnificent shafts of life.

We counted the rings in the butt of a log—132. In some periods, ten years growth added less than an inch to the thickness of the tree.

The cutters, all Negro contract laborers, are paid $2.25 per thousand feet, G. R. Prevatt told us. He supervises a crew of eight cutters, marks the trees for them, and checks their stumps. "A team of two can cut twelve to eighteen thousand feet a day in good timber," he said, "but this stand is small and thick."

After the cat drags them from the swamp, the great logs are loaded onto battered vehicles called half-tracks, trucks that have tractor belts where the back wheels should be. They haul the logs out another mile and a half, because the road is too bad for a truck to make it.

It's that kind of incredibly bad road into which the drivers throw small logs to smooth out the ruts. Loaded with the paraphernalia of photography, we rode, but we could have walked it faster and easier. Saddle soreness was the least of our ailments when we got out.

The driver of the half-track said he had begun work for Cummer and Sons last Friday, through some mistake of his own, and he was quitting next Friday. He said a month of that kind of driving would tear lose all his viscera and addle what brains he had left. He indicated he had swallowed enough dust to bring him down any minute with double pneumonia. He was from Tallahassee, and he wondered glumly what had ever brought him down into a suburb of Hades.

After a mile of this, with the driver never getting out of first gear, we shifted to a huge new Ford trailer truck. A wonderful mechanical contraption called the Logger's Dream unloaded the cypress from the half-track and placed it on the truck. This gadget is a small crane and windlass built onto a caterpillar tractor. At the end of the crane's cable is a pair of giant ice tongs. With these hooked into them, the great logs are snatched easily onto the trailer of the truck.

Here in the open there were no flies. The wire grass hinted at the waters that would come, but that was the only indication that the land wasn't a real estate subdivider's dream. Through the thin woods broad savannahs stretched away and away.

Fine pines towered among the small cypress. Along this same little road, the C. J. Jones Lumber Co. of Carnestown is hauling out pine logs—hard pine, all heart and sixteen inches thick at the butt. Cummer and Sons has a timber lease on the cypress, and the Jones Company on the pine from the owners of the land, the Collier Company.

"One good hard rain and we can't work here any more," R. T. Day, a truck driver, told us as he took us out on the last leg of the trip. "One rain will make this road pure mud, and then it'll be under water until maybe December. When that happens, we'll cut south of Monroe Station, on the forty-mile bend. We have a little railroad track going into the swamp there that we can haul on even during wet weather."

The beating that machinery was taking showed us why lumber is still high. John McElveen, head mechanic of the operation, wry and good-natured, said he'd changed tires seven times on one truck in two days. "...and half-tracks. We've ten on the job, and only three are running right now."

The price of lumber will dictate how long the cutting will continue, B. F. Cannon told us. He is the trailblazer, the timber cruiser. He first scouted the land around these operations in March 1948, but the cutting didn't begin until January 1949.

"This is Florida's last frontier," he told us, "the last stand of virgin timber. You can see why. It costs money to get this out. It's the price of low-grade cypress that gives us our profit, because only about forty percent of this timber is number one grade. Many of the trees are checked, have rotten hearts."

Mr. Cannon lives with his wife in the lumber camp by the side of the Trail. They have planted Bermuda grass around their cabin, they enjoy life there. Out there in the clearing, with the wind blowing, there were no flies, no mosquitoes, no panthers around for the moment. They were living on the edge of peace and mystery. For a moment, we were tempted.

Jane Wallace Wood
Macon, Georgia

previous page:
Baby Jane Wallace Wood, born
May 28, 1913, eldest child of
George Washington Wood, Jr.,
and Daisy Sloan Hunter Wood.

above:
Jane, here on the top step,
sits with her siblings Dorothy,
Winifred, Daisy, and George
in 1924.

right:
Jane poses for the camera in
her full Girl Scout regalia, 1924.

opposite page:
Jane and Henry Olaf Reno
marry on July 20, 1937.

7:20 a.m.
July 20, 1937

For Aunt May
— We're happier
now than we were
then. He is some-
thing rather special
as a husband.
Much love,
Jane

opposite page, top:
Exactly one year and one day after her parents' wedding, Janet Reno is born. During the next four years, Robert Marius, Margaret Sloan, and Mark Wood complete the Reno family.

opposite page, bottom:
Henry, Janet, and Jane pose for a family portrait in December, 1938.

above, from left to right:
The Reno children, Mark, Janet, Maggy, and Robert, plus cousin Nora Denslow on the pony, line up for this shot in March of 1948.

Jane Wood Reno (on the right) pushes to victory in the Cub Scout den mother scooter races, held in the early 1950s.

Jane and Henry welcome Janet home in 1952 after her year-long stay in Germany.

Photo credit: Chuck Trainor

opposite page and above:
Jane's dive into the Blue Springs is caught in freeze frame.

opposite page:
As Jane watches from a nearby rock, daughter Maggy swings into the Blue Springs of the Suwanee River.

above:
The Wood siblings reenact their early childhood portrait on the front steps. From left: Jane Wood Reno, Winifred Wood, George Wood, Dorothy Wood Denslow, and Daisy Wood Winslow.

opposite page:
The Miccosukee tribe crowns Jane honorary Seminole princess. Her Seminole name, Apoongo Stahnegee, means "messenger."

above:
Actress Lesley Woods, who portrayed Jane in the radio/television series "The Big Story," gets advice from Jane on the set.

above:
Jane (sitting to the left wearing a hat) hosts a porch party during the early sixties. Her porch became a popular meeting place for friends and colleagues, especially the Seminole Indians; the first Seminole newspaper, the *Seminole Indian News*, was created on the Reno porch.

opposite page, top:
Jane and *Miami Herald* reporter Gene Miller swap stories in 1979.

opposite page, bottom:
Janet Reno and mother Jane march in the Martin Luther King, Jr., Day Parade in 1989.

Jane cruises the Caribbean in 1991.

The front and back dust jacket photographs show Jane Wood Reno during her 104-mile, six-day hike up the beaches of Florida's east coast. Jane walked from Jupiter Light to Patrick Air Force Base, echoing the journey made by an eighteenth-century shipwrecked group searching for help.

HOW DID YOU COME TO BE NAM[ED]
PRINCESS APOONGO STAHNEGEE?

Well, later, four or five years later, in the early 1950's, the Miccosukee Indians along the Tamiami Trail organized, because the tribes, the Indians on the reservation had organized to sue the United ... money, for tre... re... l... f...

Miccosukee tribe, and I went to Washington with them, and I got drunk with them, and I went to Green Corn Dances with them, and I went to Snake Dances with them, and I wrote a lot about them.

So when they decided to make me a princess, which I think wa... about 1957 —there aren't a... in the Seminoles,

es! They just thoug... fun and I would li... wept. Smallpox To... his egret headdress a... ad, and Howard C... "Jane Wood, we ... se we like the way ..."

They decided they'd ... ncess Apoongo ... orton Silver, the la... ndian tribes, said, "... rumor bearer.'"

And I said:
"Howard!"
And Howard sa...
"Morton, don't ...
Howard Os...
"Apoongo Stah... he's a messenge... all the villages ... arrangements ... year for the G... the Snake D... ger."

But M... late it "ru... of amuse...

it. ... and I talked t... stories. I was kind of free ... wasn't working on office hours, so ... when I wrote a story about Indians I would go back and read it to them, because I early recognized that these people have a great ear for accuracy and they dislike inaccuracies far more than white people who read all these newspapers, magazines, and everything. In a I got to be an unpaid public ... selor for the

▲ When The World Gets Old ▼

From a Letter
and Uncle Bal

What interests me
would like, Uncle Bal, a
you. The Miccosukees
because most of them
English. His name is
Seminole man in his thir
person, in my experience.
school, can't read or write
he was married to a white
years, until their divorce, a
much better than any othe
He has that curious qualit
world, of being the perfec
can make of himself a ves
man's meaning to another,
anything of himself but acut
what he is trying to interpr
Seminole living in their trac
life himself, but he was raised i
is enormously interested in
and seeing it all in his own mi
ple, the traditional Seminole re
mal, intricate ritualistic panthe
rich in stories and myths.

s."
me,
man,
und to
n what
ade this
ance and
a messen-

ed to trans-
which kind

ROUND UP

June is roundup time. The new calf crop had to be branded with the "ID" of the Indian department and, often, with the brand of an individual Indian owner added to that. "Wf" is Willy Frank's brand; "7 Cross T," which he calls "7 fleur-de-lous," is Bill Osceola's brand.

Some of the cattle in the roundup had the brand of other ranchers. And these strays had to be cut out, but they were few compared with the Indians' cattle, around thirteen hundred head.

All the bulls in the Indian herd are pure-bred Brahmas. Among the many things this breed is noted for is their temperament. It is not that they are so mean—all bulls can be mean.

They are wild, they cavort and leap, they are hard to herd. They pass on these characteristics to their big-eared offspring.

Around two hundred of these calves had to be thrown, branded, and have their ears clipped. The baby bulls were castrated.

▲ Photo on previous spread: Henry Willie of the Miccosukee tribe of the Seminole Indians crowns Jane an honorary Seminole princess, Princess Apoongo Stahnegee. The Miccosukee tribe honored Reno for her work on their behalf, especially during their efforts to achieve a land settlement with the U.S. government. "Apoongo Stahnegee" translates as "messenger."

From a letter to
Aunt Peg and Uncle Bal

Written to Margaret Sloan Hunter and
Dr. Marshall Balfour, circa 1955.

Dear Aunt Peg and Uncle Bal,

We are so hoping you will have a chance to get down here before your return to India. It is a shame to be so close and not have a chance to drink a lot of coffee and talk together. Tink's Christmas card, with her girls' picture, made my heart turn over—they looked so like Nina and Tinker at that age. Fifteen Odos Deliyanni came back to me with quite a dreadful rush, because it is so long gone, and breakfasts under the pines on Odos Strofili. However, I must say I severely censure you or the Calvert school or somebody every time I get a letter from Tinker. Your penmanship instruction did not take, and her letters are a maddening exercise in decoding that cryptic script.

I don't write letters very well anymore, for the same reason ditchdiggers don't cultivate a garden in their spare time. So I don't get any, and gradually I feel spasms of remoteness that could simply be cured by some coffee together.

We enjoy your letters, my children and I. They are especially pleased to know that the elder generation of your branch of the family is staunchly liberal Democratic in politics. All my sisters and brother are Eisenhower devotees, from living with or among Republicans. Daddy and I devoutly dote on Adlai, and Bob Reno does to the extent of sending a campaign contribution of $1 to the Stevenson campaign fund. We chuckled at your last letter, saying that we must not blame Indians for not doing things our way. Hell, I think the American Republican way is often so bad in so many things, including foreign policy, that I find Nehru's path easier to champion, on the whole, than Dulles's. Dulles's difficulty lies principally, I feel, in being for so many years the minority and irresponsible party's spokesman in world affairs, that he can never learn the feel of the helm. This is, of course, true of the Republicans in general, I feel.

I have come to be, this winter, extremely interested in some Indian affairs quite close to home—namely in the Everglades. The Miccosukees of the Seminoles are engaged right now in negotiating a settlement with the United States of America, and through a series of chances and people I have come to be their unpaid public relations counsel at the moment, sort of. They are dickering with presidential representatives to get a bill through Congress for a grant of land in the saw-grass Everglades to satisfy claims that seem to have a good legal basis, or so the Bureau of Indian Affairs claims.

What interests me particularly in this, I would like, Uncle Bal, a word of advice from you. The Miccosukees have an interpreter, because most of them speak little or no English. His name is Buffalo Tiger, a Seminole man in his thirties. He is a unique person, in my experience. He never went to school, can't read or write to any extent. But he was married to a white woman for a few years, until their divorce, and speaks English much better than any other Seminole alive. He has that curious quality, so rare in the world, of being the perfect interpreter. He can make of himself a vessel to carry one man's meaning to another, without adding anything of himself but acute perception in what he is trying to interpret. He is not a Seminole living in their traditional way of life himself, but he was raised in that way and is enormously interested in understanding and seeing it all in his own mind. For example, the traditional Seminole religion is a formal, intricate ritualistic pantheistic religion, rich in stories and myths. And they have kept a verbal history of their people alive around their campfires and in their council that goes far back beyond pre-Columbian times. A few hundred, perhaps 500, of them have lived right up to now, integrated in a way of life to which we are quite alien. They have in literal truth a culture almost untouched by White men. Now Buffalo has that curious temperament that makes the greatest historians and poets. It is the impulse that makes writers, for they say it must not be that after these people die there will be no memory of them. It must not be that the world will lose all record of their dreams and stories and myths and existence as a separate people. It is the impulse first to perfectly understand, and then to write it down. Now, this man has the scholarly frame of mind. He quite understands that just because he was brought up among these people and is one of them, he does not know all about them. He is trying on weekends, for he runs a little workship in Hialeah to make a living, to—as it were—sit at the feet of the old men. Though I am not sure he has the word research in his vocabulary, he is doing research. He has, however, a good and flexible English vocabulary, and is enormously aware of the importance of the right word, the shade of meaning, accuracy. This is somewhat the way of small children, who live with a verbal history and want their stories told to them just exactly right. Now there will come a day, in a year or two maybe, when this man will feel he does know that story in the way he wants to tell it—the story of the Seminole culture, it will be. And he is going to have a problem of getting it set down. What I want to see happen is some foundation, like the Rockefeller or the Guggenheim, give him a small grant of money. That way he can buy himself a wire recorder and hire a typist to transcribe what he says. And he can take a few months off and dictate a book. It would be quite a thing for anthropology and history, and literary quality. Now, you are familiar with my enthusiasms, which do not dim. But the Bureau of Indian Affairs, and various extremely scholarly people and lawyers whom I know are just as much impressed with this project as I am. When the day comes, when Buffalo feels he is ready to try to get a book written, are there any Rockefeller Foundation grants for such a project and how does one go about getting them? Let me know about this sometime, please. If I cannot see lost causes win, I at least do not want the record of their very existence lost....

Love,
Jane

GETTING TO KNOW THE SEMINOLES

EDITOR'S NOTE: THIS IS AN OCTOBER 21, 1971, INTERVIEW WITH JANE WOOD RENO FOR THE ORAL HISTORY PROJECT ON FLORIDA INDIANS OF THE UNIVERSITY OF FLORIDA. THE INTERVIEWER IS MARCIA KANNER.

When were your first experiences with Indians?

Well, the first time is in 1950. I came to Florida from Georgia in 1925. And played cowboys and Indians as a child and Indians were so romantic to me, really, they were all romance. But I never really knew or met an Indian until I was on a dark road in a place called Devil's Garden, leading down from the road that goes from Clewiston to Fort Myers, into the Big Cypress Indian Reservation and I was stuck there with a guy named Sippi Morris in a swamp buggy and his wife and two children and my two young kids. Down the road came two truckfuls of Indians and I thought "Hmm, in the middle of the swamp, maybe they are drunk Indians, maybe I should be scared." And that's where I first met them.

Well, Sippi stepped out there and all the Indians piled out of the truck and beat him on the back and said, "Land sakes, it's Sippi!" And the white man and his wife driving the truck got out and they said, "Oh, Mr. Morris, if you only knew what's happening in the Big Cypress. There are fourteen Indian children with temperatures of 104° and we can't get any help down here. We've got some in the hospital in Clewiston but its dreadful."

And Sippi Morris said, "Well, now this Miss Wood, this Miss Reno." There was always a confusion, I wrote under my maiden name, Jane Wood, for the *Miami News*. "And she's from the *Miami News*, she tell the world all about it."

Sippi's from Mississippi. He'd been hunting and fishing with them for years. And told them more funny stories and more lies. Most Indians laugh when they see or hear of Sippi. He's pushing eighty now.

I went down in the Big Cypress. We camped out and I met Josie Billie who was, had been an Indian medicine man of the Miccosukees. And Sippi said to Josie. "Many times Josie and I have been drunk together." And Josie said "Me no drink no more, Sippi. I am a Baptist minister."

But Josie showed us Sam Jones's old town, which was at that time marked on the maps of Gulf Oil, Exxon—every oil company—as some place way off there in the middle of the Big Cypress swamp. And what it was was a hammock, where Sam Jones had camped. He had been the leader of the Seminoles where they fell back the last time into the Everglades, in trying to retreat away and away from white men. And we camped there, and then Josie Billie, about eighty, showed us where Sam Jones had been buried. Buried in a hammock, up on stone. We went there and Josie showed it to us and we looked, and there was one place that a panther had laid the night before, right beside where Sam Jones had been buried.

How long had Sam Jones been buried there?

One hundred ten years. And Josie Billie knew, right under the old cypress tree, where Sam Jones had been buried.

Would you think that they would know where other less famous Indians were buried?

Every one. But, unless you had become a Baptist like Josie had, no Indian would ever take you back to a hammock that another Indian had been buried in. Because they devoutly believe in ghosts. Buffalo Tiger told me once, "I've never seen a ghost, but my mother has."

Louise Tiger told me, "They all believe in ghosts. The time my daddy was in the hospital and then he died and then I fainted because I was pregnant; my husband Bobby Tiger came in and said 'That old man's come back to get you. That old man's come back to get you.'"

They believe in ghosts. You don't go where someone's buried, unless you become a Baptist.

What other Indians did you meet around that time? Were they all from Big Cypress?

Initially, they were around the Big Cypress, and I remember most vividly that was just a weekend, it was not where I really made friendships, though I was able to go back and write some stories—for the *Miami Herald*, oddly enough, though I was working on the *Miami News*—that brought a great deal of attention and help down to them. After all, fourteen Indian babies in the middle of Big Cypress swamp with temperatures of 104°, well, that's a pretty big newspaper story.

▲　　▲　　▲

EDITOR'S NOTE: THE FOLLOWING STORIES WERE WRITTEN FOR THE *MIAMI HERALD* IN SEPTEMBER OF 1949.

Twenty-one children—almost all of the younger generation of the Seminole Indians of the Big Cypress reservation—are seriously sick in the Sugarlands Hospital in Clewiston, stricken by a strange streptococcic infection. The epidemic fever "looks a little like measles and more like scarlet fever— you could call it a first cousin to scarlet fever," according to Dr. A. B. Johnson, resident physician at the hospital.

Contaminated drinking water on the reservation, an area of rocky, infertile swamp in a remote section straddling Hendry and Broward counties, may be the cause of the infection. Stoic Indian mothers have gone on twenty-four-hour vigils beside the beds of their children in the overcrowded hospital, where there is only one nurse on each eight-hour shift. Some of the patients have to be placed on the porch of the small hospital. Some of them lie still and listless in the quiet of a high fever, as high as 105 degrees.

Some are fretful. A rash can be seen on their faces and arms. Indian men stand quietly at the foot of their beds. The women sit next to their children— children eight months to ten years old. Their dresses are the voluminous, colorful Seminole skirts and blouses. But their faces are not Indian faces; they are mother's faces, filled with the heartbreaking expression of parental compassion and fear. The men make the sixty-mile trip from the reservation to the hospital daily, bringing food to the women.

Dr. Johnson is seriously concerned about the patients.

"With the throat infections, they are swallowing a lot of poison and it is causing them to break out in a toxic rash," he said. "There is one case of pneumonia among them and one case of pleurisy among them. Barring complications, they should all get all right, but they have been mighty sick."

The doctor said that without the help of the Indian women he didn't see how the small Sugarlands Hospital could have coped with the emergency. He went to the reservation Monday afternoon with county health officers to see what they could find out about the source of the infection.

"These Indians are good, self-respecting people," said Dr. Johnson. "They are independent and they hate to ask for help. But somebody should help them.

"The way they have to live down there is nothing to send convalescent children back to, and we will keep the children in the hospital until we think it is safe to let them go."

Miss Louise W. Bright, one of the nurses, had high praise for the Indian mothers.

"Some of the children are so sick, and the mothers are a great deal of help," she said. "Some of them speak some English and interpret for us. They help in feeding, changing the babies, and keeping them quiet."

A tour of the reservation from which the children were brought to the hospital indicated what might be some causes of the violence of the outbreak among them. The reservation is reached by the Devil's Garden road leading south from the La Belle-Clewiston highway. The last of the road is only a rutted track. The land is so rough and so sterile—miles of only rocks or swamp—that it is hard to imagine human beings gaining subsistence from it.

Raymond Henderson, manager of the reservation, and his wife talked at length about the conditions under which the Indians are living. Josie Billie, Indian Baptist minister and a resident of the reservation, and Johnny Cypress, head of one of the tribes there, discussed the children's illness and the general living conditions on the reservation with equal concern. Contaminated drinking water and inadequate medical supplies are the chief immediate concerns on the reservation, they agree.

The medical assistance provided them by the Office of Indian Affairs consists of a single monthly visit from a nurse who leaves medical supplies, they said. The office will pay the hospital bill of the children. On the entire reservation there is one well and one pump, at the house of the manager. The Indians are welcome to use that water, but instead of walking a mile or more through the swampy land, they will drink pond water, contaminated by pigs, cows, and humans.

▲　▲　▲

The battle in small Sugarlands Hospital at Clewiston against a strange streptococcus infection that has stricken the majority of children on the Seminole Indian Big Cypress reservation continued on even terms Tuesday. Three children were sent home as cured, but three more were admitted as new victims, and the number of young Indian patients in the overcrowded hospital remained at twenty-one. But Dr. A. B. Johnson, resident physician, expressed hope that the tide of battle would turn in the next few days.

"Three or four of those still in the hospital are pretty sick," Dr. Johnson said, but the others are greatly improved.

The infection, which is similar to scarlet fever, is characterized by sore throat and coughing. It takes about a week for it to run its course, followed by a week of convalescence, Dr. Johnson said. After that, it probably will take the Indian children two or three more weeks to regain their strength, longer than it should because of the conditions under which they live. Contaminated water has been suspected as the cause, but Dr. Johnson was unable to inspect the reservation because of the overload of sick children.

Kenneth Marmon, Fort Myers superintendent of the Seminole agency, Office of Indian Affairs, has sent Miss Esther Drury, visiting nurse to Indian reservations in six counties, to assist the one nurse on duty in the Clewiston hospital. The same illness swept through the children of the Indian tribes at the Brighton reservation last month, Marmon said.

"We took one child from Brighton to the Broward County Hospital. They said she had measles and refused to admit her because it was contagious."

The problem of returning convalescent children at Clewiston to their home on the Big Cypress reservation focused attention on the living conditions there. The Big Cypress reservation, with its palmetto-thatched huts, is no place for children to live. Dr. Johnson, Marmon, Resident Camp Manager Raymond Henderson, and tribal chiefs Josie Billie and Johnny Cypress all agreed on this. On the rocky swamp land of the reservation, best described as "good for nothing but to hold the world together," there is not one house for the Indians. There is but one pump, and many families are drinking pond water.

Approximately eighty Indians, counting the sick children, are now living on the reservation, though sometimes there are 150. Each family has built a camp, consisting of two or three thatched "chickees," as the huts are called. Many of the chickees have tarpaulins over the palmetto thatching, and most of them have large tarpaulins hung on the windward side to keep out a driving rain. But swamp water is never more than a few feet away. Army salvage sand fly nets hung from the peeled cypress rafters dispel any idea that Indians don't mind mosquitoes.

"Nights are damp in a chickee," Johnny Cypress says.

The immediate concern of Indians, manager, and superintendent of the reservation is care of the sick children. But a problem that is a close second in the conversation of all of them is how to live and eat at all on land that is so desperately poor that it takes twenty acres to support one cow.

A trip last week down through Oklacoochee slough, through the Big Cypress Swamp, through the Indian reservation, to within twenty miles of the Tamiami Trail, revealed the tragic scope of the Indians' problem. The two-jeep expedition was piloted by M. M. "Sippi" Morris, veteran Miami woodsman, who has been a friend of Josie Billie and Johnny Cypress for more than twenty years. Leaving the Clewiston-La Belle Highway about ten miles west of Clewiston, the jeeps cut across pasture for twenty-five miles until they picked up a sandy graded road fifteen miles north of the reservation.

This unfinished, rutted road, which comes out near La Belle, can be used by truck until it comes to the camps of the Indians some three miles within the reservation. Beyond that only jeep or canoe could manage the cattle track through the Indian territory and beyond.

Beautiful ranchland lies just south of the Clewiston-La Belle road. Deep, dark sand and improved pasture grasses make high-grade beef fat on one acre per head. But each mile of the trip south, the soil becomes thinner, more rocks crop out, the water gets higher, and pond lilies and skimpy little cypress take the place of the grass. Finally, on the Harris ranch just south of the reservation, the land must be managed so that each grazing animal has twenty acres on which to forage. It is in the heart of this country, no longer true wilderness, almost unfit for animals, that the reservation is set.

"Their hunting days are almost over," Raymond Henderson says sadly. A robust man, who usually has a twinkle in his eye, Henderson was a rancher at Davie and a Broward County deputy sheriff before the Indians persuaded him to take the job of camp manager two months ago. Between him and the Indian chiefs is the feeling of men who have found each other good hunting companions.

"The Indians, and only the Indians, can kill any game they can find on the reservation," Henderson says. "But, where a few years ago you might see six deer on a day's hunt, now you often don't find one. And where there would be twenty wild turkeys in a flock, now you find two or three. I suppose they eat as much curlew as any wild game."

"Curlew" is the hunter's name for the white ibis that still flies in clouds over the swamp land. Frogging is a seasonal pursuit of some of the Indian men, says Henderson, but they are not making any money at it, now, "And they can't sell alligator hides any more."

As for ranching like all the neighboring land owners, a very definite step has been made in that direction. On the Big Cypress reservation, ten head of cattle each have been issued to each head of ten families, a hundred in all. The scheme requires that the individual chiefs pay back cattle for each ten issued within a period of five years. Josie Billie and Johnny Cypress are both enthusiastic about the project.

Josie said, though, "I've put the heifers back to have calves, sell steers. It's good. Not enough to live on."

Pigs help in the food situation, and they run freely through the camps. They also help contaminate the ponds from which some of the tribes drink. Johnny is interested in the possibilities of commercial vegetable growing, but Marmon is dubious about the success of any commercial truck drops. It is uncertain there is any suitable land. He says that trucking the produce to market even when the reservation road is finished will be a problem, and that the capital outlay necessary to come successfully out of the highly competitive market is growing large.

Gently, sincerely, sadly, he let his hands fall open and shrugged. "Our funds are so limited."

▲　▲　▲

EDITOR'S NOTE: THIS STORY WAS WRITTEN ON DECEMBER 2, 1949. KADDY LANDRY, THE PILOT, WAS A REMARKABLE CHARACTER IN HER OWN RIGHT. SHE HAD MET JANE WOOD RENO'S SISTER, WINIFRED, WHILE THEY WERE TRAINING AS WASPS—WOMEN'S AIRFORCE SERVICE PILOTS—IN 1943. (WINIFRED WOOD WROTE A HILARIOUS ACCOUNT OF THE WASP'S LIBERATING HISTORY IN HER BOOK WE WERE WASPS.)

Mrs. Junior Buster's grin of appreciation was a wide and gold-toothed gleam when two planeloads of blankets for the Seminole Indians at the Big Cypress reservation were unloaded Wednesday by members of the Florida Air Pilots Association. Miss Kaddy Landry flew an Aeronca and a Vagabond in to make arrangements for a load of Christmas gifts to be flown to the Indians December 18 by members of the pilots' association. This writer went along to help them guess where to land.

The Dade County Park Department, through Jerry Donovan, contributed the load of blankets that was taken this trip, and when Miss Landry asked Junior Buster what the Indians needed most up there for Christmas, his first answer was, "Blankets! Last night I didn't have enough blankets!"

Taking off from Opa-locka airport, we flew above the Miami canal northwest to its second bend. Not far north of Miami it becomes a canal only by courtesy, and is really a broad green strip of water lilies stretching straight through the brown saw grass. We were flying at buzzard height, and we frightened up great clouds of white ibis that were like a miniature snowstorm.

"Fly into a flock of those and you may as well kiss yourself good-bye," Miss Landry commented.

At the second bend in the canal we turned and in ten minutes had picked up the sandy Devil's Garden road that runs south to the reservation from the Clewiston-LaBelle highway. We picked a nice, smooth-looking stretch alongside the road in the reservation, buzzed it several times to scare away the steers, and made a smooth landing on the prairie. Three hunters, gloomy about the scarcity of game this year, came along in their jeep and gave us a ride to the Seminole chickees three miles in.

There Miss Landry conferred about Christmas gifts with Junior Buster. There are about 135 Indians on the reservation at Big Cypress right now, he said, but more will probably come for Christmas. Probably fifty children are included in this number.

"Blankets, tarpaulins, mosquito nets for next summer, hatchets, axes, saws, pocket knives, and toys for the children," was his answer as to things needed for Big Cypress Christmas gifts.

Arrangements were made with Junior for a truck from the reservation to meet the planes that will fly in the gifts. These presents will be collected at a Christmas party to be given December 3 at Sunny South Airport by the Florida Air Pilots Association for all flyers and aviation enthusiasts in the area. The purpose of the gifts, Miss Landry told Junior, is to say "Thank you!" to the Seminoles who have helped pilots who have made emergency landings in the Everglades and in the Big Cypress Swamp.

Clothes, blankets, and a large supply of canned milk have been given by members of the Everglades chapter of the Daughters of the American Revolution, Mrs. William Arnott announced. These will be flown in as a DAR gift. Mrs. Murray F. Wittichen, state chairman of Indian affairs of the Florida DAR, who received many contributions for aid to the Indians following a *Herald* story about Seminole babies sick with an infection in September, will receive contributions for purchases of Christmas gifts. Material supplies may be left at the Coral Gables police station, Safety Director William Kimbrough announced.

▲　▲　▲

EDITOR'S NOTE: THE INTERVIEW RESUMES.

What happened with those children?

They got well, and they went in and put in a decent water supply. Their wells are pipes driven into the ground, and they were rather surface wells, and the water was low, so they were drinking surface water. But I met a most interesting person there. He was absolutely coal black, and he didn't speak any English. He was in his eighties. And Sippi said to me "That's the Black Sheriff of the Seminoles."

And later, many years later, I said to Howard Osceola, who is my good friend, "You remember that old black man that lived in the Big Cypress in 1950?"

"Yeah, sure."

"Sippi Morris told me once he was the black sheriff of the Seminoles."

And Howard said to me:

"That's ridiculous. That sounds like Sippi! That man was a slave of my family.

"That was a black slave of my family, and my relative—somewhere back there—had a wife who was unfaithful to him. And the first time she was unfaithful, he cut off the tip of one ear. The next time he cut off the tip of the other ear. The next time he cut off the tip of her nose. And then he thought 'Hmph.' And so he said to this black slave of his, 'My wife's no more use to me. Look, if you will kill the man that she's been being unfaithful with, I'll give her to you as a wife.' "

99
▲

"And so that black man"—that was long, long ago, said Howard— "got a shotgun, and the guy that was being unfaithful with her, he picked up a shotgun and killed him, and so she was his wife, and so he got to be a member of the tribe."

How did you come to be named Princess Apoongo Stahnegee?

Well, later, four or five years later, in the early 1950s, the Miccosukee Indians along the Tamiami Trail organized, because the tribes, the Indians on the reservations, had organized to sue the United States for money, for treaties that had been clearly and recognizably violated. But the Indians along the Trail, their fathers and mothers for generations had told them, do not ever sell your land. Well, they organized to try to get the state of Florida and the U. S. Government to make a land settlement that would be in perpetuity. It would be sixty thousand acres north of the Tamiami Trail, and nobody in the tribe could ever sell it, it could never be cut up, and it would belong to the Indians forever. And what they wanted was a land settlement.

I was writing for the *Miami News* then, and I got interested in it. I went out and talked to them, and I talked to them about Indian stories. I was kind of free-lancing, I wasn't working on office hours, so when I wrote a story about Indians I would go back and read it to them, because I early recognized that these people have a great ear for accuracy and they dislike inaccuracies far more than white people who read all these newspapers, magazines, and everything. In a sense I got to be an unpaid public relations counselor for the Miccosukee tribe, and I went to Washington with them, and I got drunk with them, and I went to Green Corn Dances with them, and I went to Snake Dances with them, and I wrote a lot about them.

So when they decided to make me a princess, which I think was about 1957 —there aren't any princesses in the Seminoles, the Miccosukees! They just thought it would be fun and I would like it. And I wept. Smallpox Tommie pinned this egret headdress around my head, and Howard Osceola said, "Jane Wood, we do this because we like the way you do things."

They decided they'd name me Princess Apoongo Stahnegee. Morton Silver, the lawyer of the Indian tribes, said, "That means 'rumor bearer.' "

And I said:

"Howard!"

And Howard said:

"Morton, don't be ridiculous."

Howard Osceola said to me, "Apoongo Stahnegee is the man, he's a messenger, he goes around to all the villages telling them what arrangements are being made this year for the Green Corn Dance and the Snake Dance. He's a messenger."

But Morton preferred to translate it "rumor bearer," which kind of amused everybody.

What kind of messages did you take back?

Well, the message that I had taken back in the intervening years, between 1950 and 1957... was that I made quite a number of friends, close personal friends, among the Miccosukees on the Tamiami Trail. These are not reservation Indians. They live on pieces of land that their daddies had staked out, or bought, or something in the 1930s, and most of them were born there, and I became very good friends with William McKinley Osceola's children, with Tiger Tiger's children. William has eight children, and very devoted, all of them. Homer, and Mittie Jim, who doesn't speak any English but makes the prettiest shirts on the Tamiami Trail, and Wild Bill Osceola, who has a daughter named after me, Jane Wood Osceola, and Howard, and Alice, who's married to a nice white man who's a stock car racer, and Ethel, who's married to a nice white man, and Ethel just had an eleven-pound baby. Her husband was extremely proud. And John, who is a charming man, and drinks! Douglas, who's the handsomest Indian in the Everglades... those are eight of William's children. He has another son, Mike, who none of them speak to, because Mike, many years ago, sued his daddy over land, and that's considered as bad taste among Indians as it is among white people.

But the Osceola family, William McKinley Osceola's children, I love them all. They have helped me out when my car was broken down, helped me through waters and swamps, I love them. Also, Tiger Tiger's children that I know are Jimmy Tiger, a very handsome man! He might be the second handsomest Indian in the Everglades, and has a fine thriving camp, and is prosperous, and of great sense of humor. He has some lovely aunts, old aunts, and old grandmothers, beautiful family.

Buffalo Tiger, who's now the chairman (it's a salaried job of the Miccosukee tribe) who's a very nice man, and I talk to Buffalo a lot. Buffalo's married to two different white women. Bobby Tiger, who's a darling man, who wrestles alligators, and has one finger bit off, and laughs and jokes, and has the prettiest daughters in the Everglades, and Bobby's wife Louise, who is half-Choctaw and half-Mississippi white person, and she prefers to live in the Everglades to Hialeah, where she and Bobby used to live.

101
▲

So anyway, along the Tamiami Trail, my personal friends are Miccosukees and they are Osceolas and Tigers.

Jane, where did these Indian names come from?

Well, Buffalo Tiger—his friends call him Buff—and I were working on a book that never came out, in 1955 or so, and let me read you from some notes from that time. This is Buffalo talking.

"When it comes to names, that was one of the things that I found hard to understand when I came to know white men. Indians don't teach their children the names of their fathers and mothers. I don't know the Indian names of my parents. Indian names are very private things. My mother's white name is Sally Willy, and my father's white name is Doctor Tiger, but these are just names for white people to use. A baby is given a name when he is born, but he is never called by this name. He's called by a nickname.

"When I was little they called me Mamusek, 'old man,' because they said I talked like an old man. When a boy successfully passes through his first Green Corn Dance he gets another name. Girls keep their same name, but they're always called by their Indian nickname. It is impolite to call anybody by their real name, though it is alright to use that name when you talk of them to some other person. You can see why I find the names of white people and the way they use the names confusing."

Well, that's what Buffalo said to me, and so you can see how confused I was and how elated, because I was in a business, newspapers—approaching public relations—where everyone wanted their name known! I thought "Wonderful people!"

What did you learn from some of these people about what it was like to grow up in the Everglades in the twenties and thirties?

Well, I'll tell you some more about what Buffalo was telling me. I'm reading from notes, but I can hear him say it now.

"I was born in the Everglades in 1920. At that time the Tamiami Trail had been built about as far as William McKinley Osceola's camp. About twenty-five miles west of Miami. My grandfather had a nice little village about two and a half miles west of where the Blue Shanty lay on the Tamiami Trail, about ten miles west of the road end. My grandfather bought skins from Indians, took them in to Miami and sold them, bought groceries to take back. He had a store in the swamp. The families of my mother's two sisters lived there, so there were many children with my sisters, and brothers, and cousins.

"My mother had ten children, five boys and five girls. Eight are still alive. Two died when they were about twelve years old. One had appendicitis, but I don't know what the other died of. My grandfather built the camp, but it belonged to my grandmother because all villages belonged to the wife. The only thing that belongs to the husband are his gun and his traps. All the children are members of their mother's clan, or family. When a man tells his wife, 'I'm going to my camp,' she knows he's going to his sister's camp or his mother's camp.

"This is the first place I know as home. Sometimes families get together, go on visits to each other. During the visits they always tell what happened in the war between the Indians and the white men, but we never see any white men. The first thing we're taught when we're little is to watch where we step, so as not to step on a snake. The next thing we're taught is to be quiet and good and mind the older people. They pointed out why we should be good. White men were the reason. They told us about the wars and how the Indians had to run off the islands in the saw grass in the Everglades, through the swamps, away from the white soldiers. A child who wasn't quiet and wasn't good might be left behind. And he would be carried back to the white folks by the soldiers.

"I can tell you, this scared you! The little ones all felt the same way at that time. They had no warm feelings toward white folks. The first white man I ever saw had stopped at William McKinley Osceola's camp on Tamiami Trail. I thought if I talked to him I would get shot or taken away from my mother. They shot guns all the time, they were always shooting something! When I was a little boy we liked to watch white men. But we were afraid to let them see us, so we'd sneak around half a day in the saw grass, just watching a man fish in the canal or watching hunters shooting guns.

"My father's work was hunting. Most of the menfolks in the village would go away from two weeks to a month on hunting trips. You know, I was so scared of white men, and then I went off when I was about twelve or thirteen to Hialeah, where my uncle had an alligator wrestling camp, you know, showing off to the white people how you wrestle alligators. I went there, and I went to school there, and I discovered that white people are just like any other people: some good, some bad."

Buff said to me—I'm really sorry it never got in print, these notes, because he said it really is important—"because these kids are growing up now, they're young punks, they won't remember anything about it." Actually, I don't think Buff's right. I think the "young punks" today will have just as great memories and stories by the time they're fifty or eighty. Their mothers and their grand-mothers and their aunts and their uncles are telling them stories too. There are a lot of them living around that are telling stories.

WHEN THE WORLD GETS OLD

In your file there are three issues of a newspaper called the *Seminole Indian News* published in August, September, and October of 1961. What were the origins of this paper? Did you have something to do with this, and is it still being published?

Best paper I ever wrote for! I loved it. This is the way it happened. In the late forties, Indians on the reservations of Florida organized as the Seminole Tribe of Florida Indians, and you had to organize to sue the U.S. Government. I believe it was in 1948 that the government passed a bill that allowed Indian tribes to sue them under violated treaties. Well, if there were any treaties ever more violated than the Indian treaties of Florida, they're just sections I'm not familiar with.

So, the Indians along the Tamiami Trail organized in the fifties as the Miccosukee Tribe of Seminole Indians, for the purpose of suing, and they got themselves a lawyer named Morton Silver. I got entranced—clear violations, what they were asking was not unreasonable, as I said, I believe, sixty thousand acres north of the Tamiami Trail to be held in perpetuity and no tribal member would own it. It would be owned by the tribe, and it could never be alienated from the tribe. And so, these are bright and sophisticated guys, even though they don't read, and Morton Silver, their lawyer, was great, and they set out to embarrass the U. S. Government. And I assisted in that.

Now this was right after John F. Kennedy...

Now, wait a minute. We embarrassed them throughout the 1950s, too. We went to—they went before I got there, ·I wish I'd been there—the United

Nations. Buffalo presented the United Nations with a buckskin declaration.

Who organized that, and when was that?

That was circa 1951 or 1952. I got in on the act in '53 and they went up to speak to the U.S. Government. The *Miami News* sent me along as a reporter, well really, that was interesting too. But it was public relations, and it was a pitch designed to embarrass the U.S. Government into straightening up and flying right. The nearest we came to success was under Leroy Collins. He came down and met with the Indians, and they came darn near to setting aside this sixty thousand acres that the Miccosukees of the Trail wanted. Except they wouldn't do it in perpetuity. They would do it du voir, thirty years, ninety years, I don't remember what.

But the state technically had the power?

Oh, yeah, it was state-owned land. They almost did it, but the Indians said, no, no term on it, it must be forever. And all ours. But Leroy came near-est doing it, and the Indians liked him. One of the most fascinating things I ever saw—Millard Callwell was associated with Morton Silver and the Miccosukees in their land claim, obviously for his potency because he was a former governor of Florida, a long-legged man, with all that Southern long-legged authority, and he came out there and gave them a pitch some time in the 1950s that they should join the Indians of the reservations in their money claim.

Those old Indians got up and talked, and talked to him through Buffalo Tiger, their spokesman. They said no, and they shamed that man, and he walked—that long-legged, arrogant ex-governor of Florida walked—down the aisle in shame. Because he had suggested, in effect, that they sell out.

What actually did you have to do with the paper, since your name appears nowhere in it?

It's well known that the rewrite man's name doesn't appear. But this paper was purely designed to embarrass the U.S. Government. It was the last gasp of the Miccosukees—Kennedy has just been elected—and it was before they dropped their land claim and decided to join the money claim. And so, Betty Mae Jumper was the editor from the reservation. Betty Mae is now the chair-man of the council. A lot of city people call her the "lady Indian chief" or something like that, but she's the chairman of the council of the Dania reser-vation, and of the Seminole Tribe. Alice Osceola was the other editor. The two lady editors met on my porch.

The editorial board consisted of Alice's five brothers, and the whole editorial board had to bring her a six-pack of beer apiece, and they would tell me what they wanted to say, and I would turn around and put it in my typewriter and read it back to them then and there. So we had a lot of fun. May I say that my great and good friend Morton Silver made it up and laid it out. He was a fascinating person, too.

This is as good as a time as any to talk about Morton Silver.

Once upon a time I was out at the Green Corn Dance about three o'clock in the morning with my daughter Janet Reno, a lovely, long-legged girl. At the Green Corn Dance you're not allowed to go to sleep, you're not allowed to eat, but you drink. So I said to Homer Osceola—Morton, and Janny, and I were there—I said:

"Homer, some day Morton will die as all men must and you're still gonna have an Indian land claim going on, and my daughter Janny Baby, who's a Harvard Law School student, can take it over."

And Homer looked at Janny and he said:

"Janny Baby, you will never make a good Indian lawyer, because you're too beautiful and too young, and you will want to be popular. Morton Silver's a Jew and he doesn't care whether he's popular or not and he makes a great Indian lawyer."

Where does Morton Silver practice law?

He practices law in Miami. I think Buffalo Tiger had come to him for a divorce or something. When I first met him everybody was saying "Eeennh! This Jew lawyer, he's trying to get in on those land claims and make all that money." His family remembers it and the Indians remember it as the time Morton was wasting all his time and not making much money at all on Indian claims. He got really roughed up. He was a crusader. And I thought to a certain extent Homer might have been right, because he was Jewish— which is a minority—and then I realized another thing. Morton had fallen out of a window when he was a boy and had to lay in bed for about a year and was crippled and had to have several operations. He was not only a Jew but he was a crippled Jew, and he was on the side of every Indian in that swamp. He waisted more time and a great deal of money, and Indians knew it. They knew it.

Now that the Indians have dropped their land claim, Morton's making quite a decent living for his six children.

The term Seminole is misleading. What does it really mean?

Well, you hear it, most books say it's "run away." But I asked Howard Osceola once: "What does Seminole mean?"

And he said:

"Well, my daddy told me that back yonder when they were chasing them all, when they were chasing all the Indians, some white soldier said to one of our fellas, one of the Miccosukees, 'Who are those Indians we see out there way away, out on the horizon? We can never catch up with them, the ones that are always running away. Who are they?'

"And our fellow said 'Seminolay!' It's a word of our language, the Miccosukee language, that means wild, a seminolay pig, a seminolay horse, wild, not fenced in, feral. It doesn't really mean run away, it means a wild hog, a wild horse—a free man!"

There are some distinctions, aren't there, between Muskogee Seminoles and Miccosukee?

That's kind of fascinating. There are remnants of two Indian tribes here now, Miccosukee and Muskogee, and they speak two different languages. But not too long ago Howard Osceola said to me, "Jane, you know, there are still some Spanish Indians in the Everglades."

And I said, "Really?" You know, the Spanish Indians, the ones we read about in history, are Calusa.

And Howard said:

"They say there are some still out there—of course this is historical legend —that don't speak any language we know. I've never seen one but my mother and daddy did. And there are supposed to be some living out there on the hammock."

But originally the Indians of south Florida had nothing to do with anything called Seminole. They were Calusas—Spanish Indians. At least it's a legend with people who are my contemporaries, a little young. But, these guys, they came down, they were two separate and distinct tribes. The Muskogees were Creeks, and the Miccosukees were initially found around north Florida, in the Panhandle north of Tallahassee. And they were pushed down and down and down, and they speak quite a different language. Their language is, their words are, not the same. They have no written language. Any written language they have is somebody's interpretation.

They're different in background entirely. When the Muskogees have a Green Corn Dance, they have to go up to Brighton and practically kidnap some of the old men to come down to sing them the chants. They're largely on the northwest shore of Okeechobee on the Brighton reservation.

I was told by Homer or Howard that in the last Seminole wars, when in effect they had become a group working and fighting together, "the Muskogees gave us the songs and the Miccosukees gave us the leaders." Osceola and Coacoochee, or Wild Cat, were Miccosukee, and they were the leaders in fighting, but the Muskogees gave them the songs. And by the way, I should tell you something about leaders. Leaders are not chiefs. These men have been more democratic than you and I could ever imagine. My own theory is—I feel it in my bones, I've read it since I knew—that they taught white American people democracy. They didn't have any chiefs. They said to Osceola, "You lead us, you fight better." There was delegated authority.

Buffalo Tiger told me once:

"All these Indians know the old stories from their side." Illiterate people. And very articulate and well-spoken people, but they don't read. "The story we know is that Coacoochee and Osceola were captured under that flag of truce when they went in, and they all went in to that place in St. Augustine, and they went in that fort. They sang a song and they made a magic, and they got the dogs quiet and they got the white soldiers asleep. And all the Indians. Coacoochee got out through those narrow little slits."

Buffalo had been up there, he said, "You know how narrow they are."

I said "Yeah."

And he said, "Osceola was too fat to get out."

So I tell that to Howard Osceola—it's a certain touching tragedy that fatness does run in the Osceola family today. They're diabetic, they can't drink anymore—and Howard said:

"That sounds like Buffalo! That wasn't true at all! Osceola and Coacoochee made a deal that Wild Cat would get out and Osceola would stay and try to reason with the white people."

It is well known that he died and Coacoochee escaped.

Betty Mae Jumper is a descendant of Coacoochee, and she told me another beautiful story. Betty Mae's about fifty, fifty-five—I think she's a little diabetic, too—and she said that if you've only got three hundred Indians, there's a good bit of recessive genes going in. You don't marry into your mother's clan, but you can marry your first cousin on your father's side, because the blood goes with the mother. And Betty Mae said:

"I was born in the Big Cypress swamp, and I'm half-white."

"You are?" I said. "Your mother or father?"

"My father was white, of course!" she said. "I'm Indian!"

Because her mother was Indian.

"When I was born," she said, "they wanted to kill me. Later I got along well enough with Cory Osceola —Cory was an old, old Indian medicine man, who I believe is dead now—but I will always remember that Cory wanted me to be killed when I was born. My grandfather picked up a shotgun and said 'Anybody bothers this baby, I will kill them.' That's why I always loved my grandmother and grandfather (they were Indians). My mother's cousin had a baby by a white man at the same time I was born. And the tribe put it out under a pine tree and stuffed its mouth full of clay and it died."

▲ ▲ ▲

Betty Mae Jumper went to college. Do you know many other Indians who have been through college?

I know of no Miccosukee Indians along the Trail—and these are the independent, nonreservation Indians that live on their own land—that have ever been to college. But, they're going to school now. And the most romantic thing happened to me when I went out to Wild Bill's camp. Some of the Indians out on the Trail live in nice cypress, board and batten houses, very pleasant houses now, a government deal. There's a pleasant school there now. Wild Bill lives near the school, but he lives in an Indian camp. Five wrecked cars, a very large ficus tree, and a great mound of beer cans around the ficus tree. I walk in and here's the older brother of my namesake, Jane Wood Osceola, sitting there. Pudgy's a very handsome young Indian of about sixteen, with a tooth broken off and long hair. Pudgy's a doll.

I had a photographer with me, and she said: "Oh! Isn't he romantic!"

"Yeah, he is," I said. "I know it."

I walked up to him and said: "Hey, she says you're very romantic. Would you consent" — he's known me since he was three feet high, and he had a twinkle in his eye — "to accepting a modeling fee of two dollars if you will sit there and let her take your picture?"

He said, "Yeah, I will, for you."

So I stepped back into the family kitchen, and it's a shack, and there's a door, and everybody in the place has written graffiti. This was last February, and there were a lot of valentines, and all the people's children's names and whatnot. But the thing that touched me most were the hearts, the hearts, and then: "Truth, Love, Honor, Jane Wood."

I thought I was going to faint! I wanted to buy the door!

Is the population of Indians declining in Florida?

Oh no, it is increasing. I had understood that after the tragic removal to Oklahoma from Tampa—the ones that did leave, and so many died, it was a trail of tears for Seminoles as well as Cherokees—there were about three hundred that fell back down into this swamp. I think one reason that I respect and love them so is because these people came from the high, clay hills that I know well, where I was born, the Appalachian hills of Georgia and north Florida, Tallahassee, those pretty high, clay hills.

They fall back down into this trapless saw grass, that was so different from their home, and to live it all seems to me a hell. Could I have done it? Live they did, and change their way of life they did. So there were about three hundred, and around 1950 there were supposed to be about twelve hundred, and now I think there are supposed to be over two thousand.

Initially I was told, back in the fifties, that Indians didn't marry until they were about thirty. But then they encouraged marriage earlier and having children earlier in recent years. I am told, and I have seen it, that if an Indian girl has an illegitimate child, nobody's mean to her. She brings it home to her mother and daddy, and they bring it up very happily, and they are not condemnatory nor censorious about premarital relationships. But once you get married, it was always supposed to be forever.

The school out there, it's not like our public schools in the sense it's compulsory education, or do you know?

I don't know. I don't believe that there's anyone out there trying to make an Indian child go to school that doesn't want to go. Generally, they're going, and they're learning English, and they speak English. Back in the olden days, the Dade County truant officer threatened to send Indians living along the Tamiami Trail to jail if they continued to refuse to send their children to school with white children.

"Why don't Indians want their children to go to school with white children?" a translator was asked.

"I asked the medicine man that," he replied. "He told me, and I translate: 'The breath-making man, that you call God, made everything different. A pine tree is always a pine tree, never a palm. If he made them different, he wants to keep the difference. The first thing an Indian child would learn to do if it went to school with white children would be to lie. The next thing would be to steal.' "

But, I find along there, with these teenage Indians, their tragedy is that they drink and drive. And the Tamiami Trail is not a safe place for that. Every

111
▲

now and then I hear of a son of a dear friend of mine who's driven in the canal and been killed. They are learning English, but you'd be surprised at the way they stay Indian.

I'm not surprised. I spoke to you before about Louise Tiger. Louise is nominally a white woman; she's half-Choctaw and half-Mississippi. She met Bobby Tiger when he was wrestling in his uncle's camp in Hialeah, and married him then. She prefers to live on the Trail. There's a great freedom... hell, those Indian boys have got their hair down to their shoulders, they're the handsomest hippies you ever saw, they'll give you the peace sign—this is what the whole hippie world's living for! Why should they run away from their families? Their families let them be like they want to be and do what they want to do.

They're staying there, living there, driving air boats, running around, driving stock cars. They run into town, but they prefer staying there. Less now are moving into the cities, I believe, than a decade ago. For example, Indian families would always take turns camping out in the center of Hialeah Racetrack. That was a job in town.

Hialeah Racetrack is the most beautiful in the world, and it has a moat in the center, and beyond the moat it has an island, upon which are some Indian chickees. During the racetrack season there are some flamingos walking about and some Indians camping there. Wild Bill camped there some time. That's a job! You go into town, camp out, cook, pay no attention to anybody, and live there for a month or two. And get pretty well paid.

They go up to alligator villages, which are tourist attractions. I used to see a lot of Indian boys parking cars in Miami. I see fewer now in town because they're making a better living air boating off the trail.

What is the Indian attitude toward women and what it the status of women in the Indian culture?

I have always, since I knew the Seminoles, had an idea that these folks that came here originally and called Indian women "squaw" and got that squaw sense were a stupid bunch of jerks who had a bad ear and brought their ear from England. In the Indian tribe it is *delegated* to the old men, you do the deciding about these kind of things, you listen to Millard Callwell, you make these decisions, you do this stuff. And with the younger men, this and this is delegated.

But Morton Silver said to me, and I got this hunch after I'd talked to him a long, long time:

"The old women do all the deciding. Their sons go home to them and say 'what would you do?'"

The blood flows with the mother. It is the mother's camp. You are your mother's tribe. Buffalo is a member of the Wind clan, which is his mother's clan. There were Wind, Panther, Frog, and Beaver clans, and the blood flows through the mother. The mother delegates the authority: husband, you go here and make the decision. I remember Janet said to Wild Bill:

"How do you know how to deliver your babies?"

Wild Bill had just delivered his fifth. He said:

"Janny Baby, my mother taught me how."

It's delegated authority. We just run the world. I felt quite at home among Indian women.

What about the image of Indian women in their chickees with Singer sewing machines?

These sewing machines came in this part of the world about 1890 with the Brickells. Not long thereafter the Indian women were making these beautiful quilted patterns which require a sewing machine. It was pedal operated then, actually it was hand operated. Now they're doing it with electric ones. I took a very perceptive writer out there once, and she was especially interested in that. She said: "I think these shirts and skirts are the only authentic Seminole craft."

"Oh, quite right," I said. "Right."

My own thesis is—I don't know where they got the quilting, it was probably circa 1900, Mary Brickell or something like that—that they made them initially so they would not be Jim Crowed. Here are these Indians coming into town, and they're dusky skinned. Our Seminoles have a pugnacious chin, and full lips, that might be Negroid. Their Indian features, the features they carried over from Mongolia, are black eyebrows, and straight black, black hair. But they are by no means red skinned. Any fool Ku Kluxer or southern immigrant might have thought they were "niggers,"and treated them badly.

So they made these shirts which said, in effect, *I am Seminole and I am an Indian.* Every little Ku Kluxer that ever came to Florida was pretty scared of Indians. They (the shirts) had no basis. They were based on the sewing machine. They were what the Indians gave the sewing machine. There's an art, and a creativity, that goes on from the sewing machine, right?

My justification is that Indians off in Big Cypress and such don't wear this stuff. They wear blue shirts and dungarees, and the women wear blouses and

113
▲

skirts of some description. Actually the young women wear blouses and dungarees. I remember in the twenties when we saw them in town, and I think we saw them in town more when we first came, they said in effect by the costumes and those beautiful blouses the Indian women wore, and the skirts, and the shirts of the men: *We are Indian*. And nobody put them down or made them sit in the back of the bus, or gave them any trouble.

▲ ▲ ▲

Tell me about Alice Jones.

Once upon a time, we were sitting out there at the Green Corn Dance, two to three miles north of Tamiami Trail. A beautiful place with a dead pine tree. Howard Osceola, Morton Silver, and I were sitting there with a bottle of whiskey and a bottle of wine, watching the dance. And Morton said: "There's Alice Jones. Have you ever told Jane Wood about Alice Jones?"

"No, I didn't," Howard said.

"What about Alice Jones?" I said.

Morton Silver, the Jewish lawyer, said: "She's ambidextrous."

"What do you mean?"

"She's a hermaphrodite, Jane Wood," said Howard Osceola, the Indian.

"Really? How do you know?"

"Well, she's a woman and she used to date our girls and she knocked them up."

"My goodness, she was a man."

"No," Howard said, "she had big breasts on her."

"My goodness, where does she live now?"

"She lives with an old, old Indian woman."

"What does Indian legend say about this?"

We'd been talking about what the Indian past said about things. Howard said:

"We never knew it before. When the world gets old, you see strange things, Jane Wood."

What ceremonials and rituals have you witnessed among the Indians? You have mentioned the Green Corn Dance and the Snake Dance.

They are two beautiful parties. The Snake Dance is later in the summer, it's late in August. It doesn't have all the religious connotations the Green

Corn Dance has. It's just a beautiful party. It's just beautiful, beautiful, beautiful. It's somewhat like the Green Corn Dance, which occurs around the first of June. Everybody's gathered on this hammock, this island, with old dead pine trees that I can still see, for a week. And they came not from miles around, but from hundreds of miles around, all Indians, Indians, Indians.

The last night of the Green Corn Dance—there were chickees set up, whole big families, seven sisters and all their brothers—nobody is allowed to go to sleep once they begin dancing. Nobody is allowed to eat. At every stop in the chanting—it's a snake-like kind of dance, hand-holding like you did in college in the twenties—they would line out the dance, three old, old men sitting there, they would line out the dance and everybody would go around. I said to Howard:

"Who's the little, little guy on the end?"

"He's my sister's son. We call him Weepers."

"How old is he?"

"Three."

This is around midnight.

"What do you mean 'Weepers'?"

"Don't you know *finders keepers, losers weepers?* We call him Weepers. That's his nickname."

Men, women, and children are chanting around, and in between every dance the Indian sheriffs walk around carrying a long, slender cypress pole, about ten feet long with a palmetto spine circle tied on the end. There are two poles, the other with a deer tail on the end.

"What do the Indian sheriffs do, Howard?" I asked.

"The Indian sheriffs make sure that anybody who gets in the dance has to take a drink when the dance stops and cannot go to sleep."

So you pass down a ritual bottle of wine, beer or whiskey. Alice Osceola was dispensing beer that night. Along towards dawn at the Green Corn Dance, everybody, not having been allowed to sleep, and not having had anything to eat for the last twenty-four hours, and having had these ritual drinks, is pretty damn drunk. It gets really pretty out there, the light, light, lightness of dawn, that pretty color.

Then what comes is a ritual scrape. They use a block of wood that's about the size of a book of matches and through it is stuck about six needles, just plain, sewing needles. They stick out about one-sixteenth to one-eighth of an inch. The medicine man goes around and he scrapes them. He scrapes their arms, their chest, and their back. Howard said they used to have a mean old medicine man that really scraped them deep. It scrapes, and they bleed.

Then they go off into small tents, where there are hot rocks, on which are thrown water. The guy sits in there and he sweats. He's been scraped, and he's bleeding. He comes out and he's covered in blood and sweat. If you walked in there at about that moment, at dawn, and hadn't ever seen it before, you would cry if you didn't know that everybody was drunk and that it didn't hurt, didn't hurt at all.

"What is this for?" I said. "Is it for health, or punishment of sins?"

"It is for health," Howard said. "A woman loses blood, but a man doesn't lose blood, so a man gets impurities. This is health. He needs a bloodletting and a sweating once a year. The punishment of sins comes later."

"What about the punishment of sins?"

"We got one here we're going to talk about tonight. There are some fellas here from that clan, fellas here from this, and one of their fellas killed one of our fellas. We're going to decide what to do."

"What might you do?" I said.

"We might take one of theirs."

"You mean you might kill the man who killed your man?"

"No," he said. "Look. This guy that got killed in our clan was a big man, he was a good man. This guy that did the killing from the other clan. You know about poor white trash," he said, "you know about poor nigger trash. Well, this was poor Indian trash. And he did the killing. So we could take not him, but one of their good guys. He killed one of our good guys."

"That's Indian justice?"

"Right."

"What are you *liable* to do?" I asked.

"We're liable to talk about it all night and not liable to do anything, and we'll leave it so if one of our guys takes one of theirs, he'll be, in effect, home free."

I'm one of the only persons I've ever known that walked out of the Green Corn Dance at nine o'clock in the morning, drove home, got dressed, and went to a Jewish wedding at noon at the Seville Hotel. The bridegroom's mother got drunk, the men danced, and I thought, boy, I've seen it all.

The Snake Dance is the same thing, but no punishment, no scraping, and just larking, just fun.

"What's the Snake Dance all about?" I asked Howard.

"Well, you know the water's high and the snakes are high. They get over the road. It's to keep the snakes quiet."

It's purely for fun. They are the most beautiful parties, and then these beautiful Indian friends of yours like Alice Osceola and Minnie Jim bring you hominy grits, fried bacon, and biscuits for breakfast the next morning, baked over a Seminole fire.

▲   ▲   ▲

The tail end of our organized Indian effort to embarrass the government of the U.S.A. came about 1960, when I was called and asked how I would like to go with a group of Seminole Indians to be a guest of Fidel Castro in Cuba. And by that time, we hadn't broken off with Fidel, but I was working for Hank Meyer Associates in public relations, no longer newspapering. I said, "Oh God, how I envy you." This was the first anniversary of Castro's revolution. "Why don't you take my son Bobby Reno, who is working on the *Miami Herald?*" I said.

So they took Bobby. They had the thirteenth floor of the Hilton Hotel, and Bobby said it was the wildest and most beautiful weekend. The crowds and everything, and all the Indians, including me, he said, were on the balcony with Castro and he kissed us with the tears streaming down his cheeks. We all got drunk on champagne on the thirteenth floor of the Hilton, he said, and those Indians can drink up a storm. That was the last gasp, in effect, of the Miccosukee Revolution of 1950, which was a public relations revolution, an attempt to embarrass the U. S. Government into behaving. I always wished I'd been there.

ROUND UP

The blat of outraged calves, bawling steers, cherry-red branding irons, battered Stetsons and faded Levis, high-heeled boots with rowelled spurs looked over the fence rail of the corral—every mark of the Old West was there.

Over it all hung the authentic stench of roundup time—the acrid smell of burning hair and the sick-sweet smell of burning flesh, and the smell of hundreds of cattle jam-packed and milling together.

But rimming the picture were not high purple peaks or Texas plains. The background was a wall of feathery light-leaved cypress.

Under the Stetsons were copper-colored faces. The full, long, gaudy skirts of the Seminole were draped over the top of the rail of the high corral as the Indian women perched there between the cowboys and their sloe-eyed children.

It was roundup time at the Big Cypress Seminole Indian Reservation.

West is East, the twain meets, and the Indian plays cowboy.

So many of the details of the roundup seemed too true. There was no chuck wagon, no guitar, and nobody rolled his own cigarettes. But occasionally a clear call, "Yi-yi-yippi!" came rolling right out of the Lone Ranger.

(And some of the Indian women, as they sat and sewed on their hand-run Singer sewing machines in their sleeping chickees had battery-operated radios blasting away.)

Ponchos in a neat roll were tied on the backs of the saddles of authentic cow ponies. Once during the sweating afternoon, the ponchos had to be brought out as the welcome flurry of a Florida squall cooled the packed herd.

June is roundup time. The new calf crop had to be branded with the "ID" of the Indian department and, often, with the brand of an individual Indian owner added to that. "Wf" is Willy Frank's brand; "7 Cross T," which he calls "7 fleur-de-lous," is Bill Osceola's brand.

Some of the cattle in the roundup had the brand of other ranchers. And these strays had to be cut out, but they were few compared with the Indians' cattle, around thirteen hundred head.

All the bulls in the Indian herd are purebred Brahmas. Among the many things this breed is noted for is their temperament. It is not that they are so mean—all bulls can be mean.

They are wild, they cavort and leap, they are hard to herd. They pass on these characteristics to their big-eared offspring.

Around two hundred of these calves had to be thrown, branded, and have their ears clipped. The baby bulls were castrated.

Then the whole lot—outraged calves, their bawling dams, the long-horned steers, and the strange great Brahma bulls with their monstrous looking humps—had to be driven through the dipping vat.

The reservation is a tick-free area. That means it is officially free of the particular tick that carries cattle fever. But the cattle are dipped to rid them of lice, wood ticks and other parasites that pull down their weight and give them rusty coats.

Two weeks before the roundup the Indians had built the big corral out of the slender cypress that grows through their "ranch" by the million. Done with axe, hatchet, hammer and nails, it was a stout, workmanlike job, with the three-inch-thick log rails reaching higher than a man's head.

Morgan Smith was a great brown impassive Buddha as he directed and helped in the operations, but a Buddha that was fast on his feet. Jimmy and Junior Cypress were there as cowboys.

These three are the trustees of the Indian cattle enterprise. They are nominated and elected by their own people, meeting in a body, and they hold office for three years. A new man is elected each year, and he can be reelected if everybody is satisfied with his work.

Smith has been working with cattle around Lake Okeechobee since 1915, and the Cypress boys know their stuff, too. Willie Tiger brought his considerable experience as a cowboy down from Brighton reservation to help out.

But to the other Indians who were working as cowboys the day of the branding, the whole business was fairly new. They had about them the air of the willing amateur. There was a good bit of laughter and a game-like air about their calf "rassling."

Raymond Henderson, white camp manager of the Big Cypress reservation, was keeping tally down in the corral during the branding. Half Henderson's salary is paid by the Indian agency, half by the Indians themselves out of the funds of the cattle association.

He is a husky man, with a slow flashing smile and a twinkle in his eye that leads Indians to name their sons after him. Before he took the job at the reservation as camp manager last year, he had ranched for years near Davie.

Fred Montsdeoch, white agricultural agent for all the Seminole tribes in Florida, was there to help out, sweating and advising.

But since the best of the sixteen Indians who were working as cowboys were not what anybody would call professionals, they got a good deal of fun and laughter out of it. For men who eat far more curlews and garfish than they do beef, they pitched in and dragged the bawling calves down by their heels with a right good will.

They were paid six dollars a day by the cattle association for their work in the roundup. If they worked on horseback, there was another $1.50 for the horse.

A handful of women and children were there. One pretty young Indian woman, balancing athletically on the high rail, laughed and joked until operations got under way. But when she saw the work being done on a bawling calf just beneath her, her tight-shut eyes and squinched-up face said more plainly than words, "I can't bear to look!"

Part of the afternoon's work consisted in assigning to three Indian men ten calves each that will be their own stock and will form the nucleus of a herd that may make them one day self-supporting. The deal is that each man returns to the association, at the end of six years, eleven calves to pay for the ten he was originally given. His range, the thousands of acres of the swampy reservation, is free. It is already fenced.

If these men who through the years are receiving cattle from the association stick to a steady diet of gopher turtle, manage their stock well, and have luck, they should be able to pass on to their sons a herd that will make them cattlemen.

Any tribesman on the Big Cypress reservation may apply for these calves. The trustees and the Indian agent, Kenneth Marmon, make the decision as to how many can be distributed and who shall receive them.

"They handle the trusteeship well, with mighty little bickering—work together good," Henderson says.

There will not be another distribution of calves until 1952.

So Willie Frank and Bill and John Osceola, who got ten calves each, were in the corral working away. Morgan Smith would point out one and say, "Willie!" and Frank and another fellow would flatten him out, while two helpers hurried with the branding irons, the "ID" and the "WF55." Then Smith with a razor-sharp pocket knife would slice a new moon out of one of the calves ears, and slit the other one for three inches.

Each man makes individual cuts in the ears of his cattle to identify his stock in the fall and winter when their hair is so long the brands cannot be seen.

After all these operations on the bawling little creatures is over, they have to be kept in a fenced pasture for a week or two and watched closely for screw worms. This is one of the great pests of the Florida range. A fly may lay eggs in any open wound, and the maggots that hatch work in and into the animal until they hit a vital spot and it dies. Smearex is the U.S. Department of Agriculture's weapon against screw worms, and there are half a dozen other preparations that will kill them, but a cattleman has to watch his animals like a hawk to catch the pest in time.

The entire cattle enterprise is a business and not a subsistence project, Henderson explains. The association is building up a source of money for the tribe, and so there's not much beef-eating.

"They may kill a steer for a barbecue at Christmas and a few other big occasions, but they'd have few left if they ate them regularly," he says.

The project began in 1939, when the Indians of the Big Cypress took tribal money coming to them from the cattle enterprise at the Brighton reservation, and stocked the big Cypress reservation. Some have been bought and some sold since then.

To anybody who has driven through that reservation in a rainy fall, with every road hub-deep in water, the range in early summer looks like one version of paradise. Where 80 percent is flooded in wet weather, 80 percent is high and green in the dry.

Perhaps 40 percent of the better range of the reservations is in slender, lacy-leaved cypress, and the other 60 percent is in open grassland—a few inches of sand and some marl over rock. The timber is no good to the lumber companies, being small and heart-checked, but it is perfect for the framework of the thatched chickees, for fence poles, for corrals.

The word in that region is that the Seminole is well liked by the white hunter, disliked by the white rancher and cowhand. Hunters who have gone out with them are quite positive why they like them, because they are good hunters, good campers, good-natured and good companions. And they're honest. You can leave a jeep full of hunting equipment anywhere on that reservation for a week and everything will be just like you left it when you come back.

The answer to why the cattleman dislikes the Seminole is harder to find.

One white man sitting watching the branding on the corral fence said, "I don't know anybody else has it so easy. Willie Frank there is being given ten calves, and he's got his range all free and fenced. He ought to be able to make something of it."

A short memory can forget how Willie Frank's people got the land.

Josie Billie, a tribal trustee who is sixty-four years old, was reminiscing about how his family came there. "I was born near Jacksonville. My grandmother was born near what is now Atlanta, Georgia. We didn't come down here all in one trip, came a little at a time, after the war."

Casually he said, "the war," as though it were yesterday's war, to the only war.

"Which war? Oh, the Indian war, 'bout 1830."

Willie Frank, who had a fine time playing cowboy in the corral, went to his mokalee that night and ate gopher for supper. The live gopher turtle had been placed in the coals of the cooking fire until it stopped sputtering and then pushed well in to roast. When his wife figured it was done she raked it out and set it aside to cool. That night he pulled out a leg at a time and ate the meat.

His "mokalee" is home, the clearing that holds two or three "chickees," the palm-thatched huts. "Immokalee" is "my home."

They play Indian, too. A beautiful, dungareed, dark little five-year-old stood under a palmetto on the edge of his mokalee and ineptly practiced with a clumsy bow and arrow. Josie Billie says he has no memory of a bow and arrow being used as a weapon among his people. It was a toy to that Indian boy, every bit as much as it is a toy to your child under a palmetto in your backyard.

123
▲

BLACK MARKET BABIES

Driving a borrowed Cadillac, wearing a phony diamond ring, I went out to buy babies on the black market for the Kefauver committee.

No baby sellers that I found here have any ready for immediate delivery, but I have ... newborn ... 2,000 to ... ow.

... call me ... will be ... mild- ... Cole, ... sell- ... after- ... llers ... rod- ... help ... ves ... al

... he asked me to ... "... thoughts fly out the window, they forget they might be investigated."

... You drive up in a Cadillac, people's ...

Mitler gave me names. One of them was Dr. Katherine Cole, a naturopath. I looked up her record and found that she had been convicted of murder in the third degree in the death of a woman following an abortion. The conviction was reversed by the Supreme Court because of insufficient evidence. Due to the fact that the woman who said Dr. Cole performed the abortion died, it was not proved that the woman knew she was dying.

Dr. Cole was also, I found, once charged with failure to file a birth certificate in a case ...

BEACH WALK

For six days I walked 104 m
up the beaches of the Florida
coast, from Jupiter Light to Pat
Air Force Base. Two nights I
on the beach, walking on bet
naps.

In a bag slung on one sho
carried cheese, raisins, and be
pers, water in a plastic o
detergent bottle, a bug-bomb
light water-repellent jack
hood, a plastic bag to keep
warm, plenty of matches,
comb, Kleenex, a map, li
enough money.

After noting on the fi
I could skinny-dip in cc
vacy almost anywhere
beach, I left my bathin
to lighten the load and
to regret it until the la
reached a populated k

The idea that w
beach would be a

COOPS

Mrs. Vivian Womack got her divorce from Lew Womack on December 30, 1953. On January 4, 1954, married a blonde cocktail lounge hostess named Jackie.

On July 23, 1954, Womack died in the explosion of the new motorboat he had built from a kit given him by his new wife.

Pete Balma, his partner in policing and allegedly in crime, got a divorce from his wife and married the second Mrs. Womack, Mrs. Jackie Womack, on January 4, 1955.

When Womack married Jackie they lived with his mother, Mrs. Grace Womack, for a while. Womack bought furniture and got his mother to give her old furniture to the Salvation Army, says his sister.

And he told his mother that when he and his new wife got a home of their own, the furniture was to be hers.

But when Balma and Mrs. Jackie Womack left Mrs. Womack's house after they were married, they took all the furniture and left her nothing but a cushion to sit on, says Womack's sister.

Mrs. Jackie Womack collected the insurance from the death of her husband of six months.

▲ Photo on previous spread: This 1982 photograph shows Jane surrounded by some of the most important headlines of her era. Here she sits among memorabilia of her journalistic career.

SCOOP

A Miami uniformed policeman was arrested last night by Chief Walter Headley as the fingerman in a series of holdups.

The action stemmed from a statement by a state prisoner at Deland who related a weird story of a tie-in between two Miami policeman and a "stupid group of thugs" from New Jersey.

The arrested policeman is Pete V. Balma, age twenty-seven.

Implicated by the prisoner's story was Officer Lewis Womack who died in the mysterious explosion of his sixteen-foot motorboat in Biscayne Bay on July 24, 1954. Since then Officer Balma has been divorced from his wife and has married Womack's widow, Jackie.

In split-second timing based on information relayed back from the prison by Captain Chester Eldredge, Chief Headley also directed the arrest of Gerald Casselli, age forty-two, of 300 NE Sixtieth Street, said by Eldredge to be head of the police-thug operation, and of Ralph Tango, a henchman of the gang.

Chief Headley personally took Balma's pistol, badge, and equipment from him.

The confession that led to the roundup was made to me.

It was immediately repeated to Captain Eldredge and to Miami Detective Charles Sapp. The three of us left Miami at 4 A.M. yesterday in an eighty-mile-an-hour dash to the Florida State Prison Camp at Deland.

Leroy Horne, thirty-five, of Miami, who is serving a ten-year sentence for armed robbery there, told Captain Eldredge, Sapp and myself the complete details of four holdups and one theft that he had committed with this gang.

Horne said he did this to lift the burden of anxiety from his twenty-four-year-old wife, Irene, who had their third child two months ago.

"It was a little girl, and she is so beautiful," her father explained.

He did it without asking or getting any promise of leniency, to try to straighten out the tangle of his past and to stop the activities of the frightening policeman-steered gang he left free when he went to the penitentiary for ten years for armed robbery last fall in a sentence passed by Judge Ben C. Willard.

Judge Willard's kindness to Horne's then-pregnant wife—raising money to send her to live near her husband—and an article in the *Miami Daily News* last fall about the tragic plight of the mother and her two small children led to Horne's confession. The kindness of the people of Deland, where his wife moved to be near him, helped. He has become a member of the Presbyterian church there.

Word came that Horne wanted to talk to me. I took an outline of what he wanted to talk about to Chief Headley. He assigned Captain Eldredge to the case with the full facilities of the police department.

Eldredge went after the answers in a thirty-six-hour stint of exhaustive and exhausting investigation of all the leads Horne supplied. The result was an arrest of the men pointed out as kingpins in Horne's story of a bunch of sordid and dangerous men.

Eldredge's burn was blue hot.

The captain and Detective Sapp did not sleep until they got policeman Balma in jail last night.

When Eldredge, Sapp and I went to Deland to talk to Horne, he was happy to see somebody he could tell all about his share in a series of holdups.

A former TV repairman, he adjusted and got going the tape recording machine on which we recorded his detailed confession of holdups and a theft in which he participated.

They were:

A holdup of the Gulf Life Insurance Company on February 18, 1954, in which he and Jerry Casselli gained about three hundred dollars.

A holdup of E. H. Dine in the Preview Lounge on Coral Way on April 25, 1954, in which he and Jerry Casselli gained about three thousand dollars.

A theft from a general mercantile and hardware store in Ft. Lauderdale, sometime in June or July of 1954. He forgot the name of the store, and forgot the amount taken, but he remembered the method of operation in detail.

A holdup of Harold and Haygood Brick Company in Ft. Lauderdale, in which his crew netted less than two hundred dollars in June or July of 1954, shortly after the mercantile store theft.

In addition, Horne outlined the way in which patrolman Pete Balma set up and suggested various targets for these stickup activities. For his services, Horne said, the policeman was paid 25 percent of the gross take by the New Jersey drifters.

Apparently, said Horne, Balma's policing partner, Lewis Womack, was also a partner in the holdup planning during the period within which Horne was familiar with the gang's activity, between February 1954 and October 1954.

Balma, Womack, and Jerry Casselli conferred over all of the Dade County holdups, over coffee at Casselli's home on NE 60th Street or in a drive-in restaurant, Wimpy's, in the southwest section.

Horne says that he was told by Casselli that Balma got 25 percent of the gross take for his planning activity with the group.

However, said Horne, in his account of gang activities, on at least one occasion Balma took an active part in the gang's stickup work. This was in a first holdup of the Gulf Life Insurance Company, sometime before the second hold-up of the Gulf Life Insurance Company.

On the way to this robbery, Jerry and the holdup helper told Horne that they had stuck up the same company previously. On that occasion he said they told him that Pete Balma, the policeman, was one of three men who held guns in the side of a man who came out of the insurance company office with a satchel. The man gave up to them the money-loaded satchel without a word.

Horne did not explain whether on this occasion the officer got more than his usual 25 percent for planning the robbery.

Sorry planners they all turned out to be. Horne said that Balma, five or six times in the months before the holdup of the Preview Lounge on Coral Way on April 25, 1954, had suggested to Jerry that the wandering crew of gunmen stick up this place.

The Sunday before the Sunday of the actual holdup, Jerry Casselli spent some two hours with Dine, owner of the Preview. Jerry, said Horne, was dressed up and pretending to Dine that he wanted to rent the lounge.

The ringleader had word from his policeman confederate, said Horne, that on any Sunday two or three hours before the opening of the place, there would be several thousand dollars in the office of the lounge.

After Jerry's "casing of the joint," he returned for the actual holdup the following Sunday. Of the thousands promised by their police tipster, he and

Horne got only three hundred dollars on that job.

It was after the Harold and Haygood Brick Company job in Ft. Lauderdale, said Horne, that he really began to lose confidence in the information that the police informant was passing on to Jerry. On that job, a payroll was promised, but instead there was less than three hundred dollars in the two boxes he and a henchman of Jerry's took from the brick company.

All these men called each other continually by their first names. That is why last night Eldredge had crews combing the town for some of the members of the group. Horne simply did not know some of the last names of the men who were very familiar to him as members of the holdup crew.

Sapp said when he left Horne walking very straight back to the prison quarters in Deland, "I would be willing to bet that every last thing this fellow told us is completely true and accurate."

Eldredge and this writer agreed with him.

In all the time the group was operating in Miami with Horne as a member, he said they used only phony guns in their "armed robberies." They were air pistols that looked like Lugers. They could not hurt anybody, but they could scare them, he pointed out.

Horne was mild, reflective, and unembittered in his accounts of gang activities. He had, he said, expected them, when he went to the penitentiary without talking, to give his wife 25 percent of any future holdup proceeds they would net. He indicated that he thought now it was very stupid of him to have expected any such thing from his fellow night workmen, because they had been quite unable to raise the $750 bond for him to get out of jail.

He was caught in a holdup of the City Loan Company, 5996 NW Seventh Avenue. His cohort, Jerry, was at that time a driver of a Budge Hardware Company truck. Horne was supposed to go into the office and do the holdup and run out and escape in his car.

Behind him, the "brains," Jerry, was supposed to follow closely in his truck to cover Horne in case of any pursuit. Horne ran out of the loan company with his loot. A young man ran out of the company and spotted him as he pulled away in his car. Horne turned a corner and went to his house, and the young man followed. When this young man found the hole in which his quarry had fled, he also found he was just around the corner from Justice of Peace Edwin Lee Mason's office.

So the pursuer went around to Mason, rallied the law, and nabbed Horne with the loot.

Jerry told Horne's wife afterward that he had been stopped by a red light in his efforts to block Horne's trail. Horne said yesterday that Jerry could not have been blocked by a red light, that he was parked all ready and handy in his truck.

But Horne indicated he felt he was a fool ever to have listened to the first proposition from Jerry and that he was no greater fool for expecting Jerry to efficiently protect him in a holdup.

The picture Horne drew of Casselli was of a flabby, ineffectual, foolish man, unable to coherently organize their lives in a sensible way.

The men with whom he did the holdups went to jai alai or dog tracks and gambled away forty to sixty dollars a night. They grabbed thousands that didn't belong to them, yet their automobiles were repossessed because they did not meet their payments.

Horne seems to be completely honest in considering himself worse than a fool to have been enmeshed in and ruined by this life. He is not blaming anyone. But he gives his young wife, who is now living on seventy-one dollars a month paid to her by the state, entire credit for pulling him out onto an island where he could look at himself and at these other men.

While Horne is in jail and Balma, Casselli and the others are under arrest, Lew Womack is dead.

The Miami Police Department ruined Lew Womack. He was a wonderful fellow until he got to be a policeman. It was the low pay, the men he got to know, and too many chances to be crooked.

This is the summary of the life of a man who was blown up in a boat explosion last summer and in death was accused Saturday as one of two policemen who planned a series of robberies with a holdup gang here in the last two years.

The woman who describes him this way still loves him. She is Mrs. Vivian Hurley Womack, his first wife. She met the handsome young Miami High athlete first when he came to her home town of Salisbury, North Carolina, as a baseball player. She married him in 1941.

She divorced him December 30, 1953, because, she says, she hated what he did in his four years of working for the Miami Police Department.

He was unfaithful to her and he was crooked, she says.

She loved him, but she could not stand their life together any longer.

Womack's sister, Mrs. Mildred Cline, of Hialeah, says the same thing. "I never knew that Lew was crooked," she says, "but he changed in the four years after he went to work for the police. This is horrible for my mother."

And Lew Womack's mother, whose other son is a minister, says nothing and grieves. For her son lost his life—and now his reputation.

He was a good baseball player and he made a handsome, steady husband for the first ten years of his married life to pretty, dark Vivian Hurley.

He had a job with Pan American and then he was in the Coast Guard—and then he doesn't look so wonderful, she says, because he didn't do a very good job of helping support her while in the service.

But he was faithful and he was honest, as far as she knew. In 1950 he joined the Miami police force. She didn't want him to take the job because even if he was "wonderful," she knew by then he wasn't of stainless steel character.

Once, when she was sick and he told her he didn't have a cent of money for her, she happened to look under the floor mat of the car and found one hundred dollar bills in a roll there.

"So, I knew he was into something bad," she says, "But the only thing I ever knew he did crooked for sure was when he and Pete Balma were riding together."

Balma is Womack's policeman partner who was arrested Saturday as fingerman for a holdup gang.

"I came out in our car," says Mrs. Womack, "to Edison Center, and Pete and Lew were loading a lot of stuff out of the Black Maria into our car (a Black Maria is an official police vehicle). It was a lot of automobile equipment. They had found an open warehouse.

"It was too much for me. And then I found that Lew was living in the southwest section with a blonde woman and he was introducing her as Mrs. Lew Womack. I'm a brunette and I was living in Hialeah. He was never at home at night with me, not after he became a policeman.

"Two years ago I had to have an operation for a toxic thyroid. If I had gone a few more months, the doctor said I would be dead. There were a lot of debts, but I couldn't go on with Lew anymore.

"It hurts when you still love a man, to throw all those years over your shoulder by getting a divorce. He didn't want me to, and he contested it."

Mrs. Vivian Womack got her divorce from Lew Womack on December 30, 1953. On January 4, 1954, he married a blonde cocktail lounge hostess named Jackie.

On July 23, 1954, Womack died in the explosion of the new motorboat he had built from a kit given him by his new wife.

Pete Balma, his partner in policing and allegedly in crime, got a divorce from his wife and married the second Mrs. Womack, Mrs. Jackie Womack, on January 4, 1955.

When Womack married Jackie they lived with his mother, Mrs. Grace Womack, for a while. Womack bought furniture and got his mother to give her old furniture to the Salvation Army, says his sister.

And he told his mother that when he and his new wife got a home of their own, the furniture was to be hers.

But when Balma and Mrs. Jackie Womack left Mrs. Womack's house after they were married, they took all the furniture and left her nothing but a cushion to sit on, says Womack's sister.

Mrs. Jackie Womack collected the insurance from the death of her husband of six months.

When the first Mrs. Womack got a divorce, Lew Womack put a second mortgage on her home to pay the accumulation of doctors' bills from her illness. As the divorce settlement shows, he promised to pay half of the fifteen-hundred-dollar second mortgage. Womack paid nothing toward the debt before his death, and none of the insurance was applied to it.

"Lew and Pete Balma," says Mrs. Vivian Womack somberly, "thought they were the only smart people in the world. They thought everybody else was stupid."

"Policemen," says Mrs. Vivian Womack in her bitterness, "are looking for something for nothing. But can you blame them too much? The city is trying to get something for nothing in the pay they give policemen."

A beginning policeman draws $260 a month.

BLACK MARKET BABIES

Driving a borrowed Cadillac, wearing a phony diamond ring, I went out to buy babies on the black market for the Kefauver committee.

No baby sellers that I found here have any ready for immediate delivery, but I have the promise of a newborn infant next April for somewhere around $2,000 to $3,000 with a $500 cash down payment right now.

Another cheaper baby dealer promised to call me when he gets an unmarried mother and his price will be a little more than $1,000.

Among the baby sellers in Miami is a little, mild-mannered, grandmotherly woman, Dr. Katherine Cole, who has left behind her a trail of death. The man selling babies cheap is Dr. Eduardo Suarez.

Wild comedy, sheer terror, death on a Sunday afternoon—all these you find among the strange baby sellers who have flourished here for years. They are the products of a city—Miami—that does not give enough help nor kindness to unmarried women who find themselves pregnant.

"Take my Cadillac, " said Ernest Mitler, special legal counsel of the Kefauver committee when he asked me to buy babies for him. "You drive up in a Cadillac, people's thoughts fly out the window, they forget they might be investigated."

Mitler gave me names. One of them was Dr. Katherine Cole, a naturopath. I looked up her record and found that she had been convicted of murder in the third degree in the death of a woman following an abortion. The conviction was reversed by the Supreme Court because of insufficient evidence. Due to the fact that the woman who said Dr. Cole performed the abortion died, it was not proved that the woman knew she was dying.

Dr. Cole was also, I found, once charged with failure to file a birth certificate in a case where she arranged to have two babies born in different places, of different mothers, registered for a birth certificate as twins. This case was "nol prossed." ("nolle prosequi", not prosecuted)

I drove the Cadillac to Dr. Cole's clinic at 4765 SW Eighth Street. It is a very long car. The little wire-recorder in my pocketbook, a thing called a minofon, makes a whirring noise and has to be handled as gently as a sack of eggs. Both made me so nervous my hands shook and my voice trembled. Dr. Cole was very kind and gentle to me.

"I'm Mrs. Frederick Zimmerman," I told her, "and I was down here on a fishing trip with some friends, when my husband wrote me that we might be able to adopt a baby in Florida. He said some New Jersey people gave him your name. My husband, Zimmy, is perfectly wonderful, and he can give me anything in the world I want. But we can't have a baby. And the social workers won't let us adopt a baby."

Dr. Cole showed me a picture of her five children, and told me she was deserted by her husband, a brilliant man, and her professor in naturopathy, when she was twenty-four years old. Her husband ran off with his secretary. Her family wanted her to bring the children back to the big South Carolina farm where she was raised. But she could not, and then and there she resolved that she would never let any baby she delivered in her obstetrical practice be put in an orphan's home.

"I just placed a lovely baby with a New Jersey couple recently," she commented.

I took off my white gloves, her glance brushed the ring on my hand, and we started talking figures. The stone in the ring is a zirconium, with a higher index of refraction than a diamond, not quite as big as a Cadillac headlight. Dr. Cole perceptibly relaxed.

"All that the social workers at the welfare board will let me charge adopting parents," she said, "is a delivery fee, $150. But it is too tragic and hard for poor girls who are expecting illegitimate babies to have to go through all their pregnancy without help, when they won't let their families know their condition. So I take care of the girls from the time they first come to see me."

She has a lovely eighteen-year-old girl staying with her right now, she said, and looked in her card index. The girl is going to have a baby between April 25 and May 10. The father is a boy going to the University of Miami.

Dr. Cole said she would expect my husband and me to pay the girl's expenses and to pay enough to send the girl away with a little money so that she will not be destitute. She suggested I pay her some then, and the balance when the baby is born.

"How much?"

"Five hundred dollars now, and the balance will be the amount I spend on the girl, when you and your husband fly down from New York next April to get the baby," she replied. "I'll keep a record of everything I spend on her."

"About how much will the balance be?" I asked.

"I don't know," said Dr. Cole, "because I don't know what it will cost me to take proper care of the girl. Sometimes there are x-rays and things that run up the cost."

"Would it be $2,000 or $3,000?" I asked. "Zimmy, my husband, won't mind. But I do think he would like to have some sort of idea," I told her.

"I don't think it will be that much," said Dr. Cole, watching me very carefully, "but if it is, will you and your husband quibble about the money?"

Zimmy quibble? No quibbler, he! I told her.

I would never know the mother's name, and the mother would never know my name, Dr. Cole assured me. The total amount we paid would include hospital fees and various living expenses of the girl, who did not want her parents to know anything about her condition.

"When you finally pay me when the baby is born," Dr. Cole explained, "I'll want you to give me part of the money in cash and the rest as a check. We'll work out the amounts. That is so you and I can both say to the welfare people that the check is all you paid me. You mustn't tell them about the balance in cash."

The minifon in my pocketbook was making me so nervous that I cried a couple of times during our visit. We parted in a glow of mutual esteem. I was to wire Zimmy in New York for the $500 and return.

"I can't give you a receipt for that money," Dr. Cole cautioned me. "You will have to trust me."

Next day I returned to the plump, gentle little elderly woman, to tell her that Zimmy wanted to fly down next week to discuss with her whether the adoption would be legal.

"You don't need to worry," she assured me. "New York laws are terrible. What you should do is adopt the baby here. Come here about a year after you take the baby and establish legal residence. You won't have any trouble in adoption, it will be perfectly legal. The courts never take the baby away from people who already have it. I have the best lawyer. He will draw the papers for the girl to sign, and he will work with your New York lawyer to get the legal adoption here. A couple came here from Springfield, Massachusetts, and got a lovely baby with no trouble at all, recently."

We chatted on the subject of morals, which are no worse today than they were fifty years ago, Dr. Cole said. She remembered back to the days of her childhood on a South Carolina farm. I remembered back to the days of my childhood on a Georgia farm and almost pulled a picture of the four children I really do have out of my pocketbook to show Dr. Cole. Just in time I remembered the minifon.

"I never coerce a girl to give a baby for adoption, but once they agree, they seldom renege. I can tell. I try to persuade these girls, when their parents are people of substance and well able to take care of them, to tell their parents. I remember telling a girl, 'If you would let your parents know the trouble you are in, they would be staunch.'

" 'My mother would drop dead,' the girl said.

"I don't think so, or there would be a lot of dead mothers in the street," said Dr. Cole.

As I was leaving, we discussed our Cadillacs. Dr. Cole drives a 1955 Fleetwood, with more assurance, I am sure, than Mrs. Frederick Zimmerman.

So, if I had been what I said I was, Dr. Cole would have seemed to me an angel. Her judgment in placing a baby with an amateur investigator for the Kefauver committee is not good. But, I thought, is not her danger ignorance, and her intention good?

The next day I talked to a woman Dr. Cole "helped" to have a baby. I saw the road to Hell these good intentions pave. Call the woman Louise Young, because that is not her name.

"Dr. Cole helped me, yes, in 1953. She gave me a month's rent after my baby was born. It was $12.50 a week, about $48 she gave me in all. And she didn't charge any delivery fee."

Was she kind?

"No, she delivered me in an ordinary bed in what must have been a bathroom at one time. She didn't seem to be thinking of me at all, she was just thinking of the baby. She shouted at me.

"I didn't see my baby. She wouldn't let me see it at all. Just said it was a female. She said it was better that way. She and the nurse practically said I had to sign the papers before I came to very well. She gave me a little something, ether, I guess, that knocked me out right at the end. The nurse held my hand so I could sign the papers giving up the baby.

"Before I had gone around town trying to get help from all the social agencies. I couldn't work and I needed a place to stay. The Salvation Army wanted me to go to Tampa to the Florence Crittenden Home there, but they couldn't think of a way to get money to send me. The Family Service didn't seem to know of any help for me. Then I went to the state welfare office in Coconut Grove. I always wondered if they sent me to Dr. Cole."

A few days after her visit to the welfare board office, a tall, dark, young man named George came to see her and said he was a lawyer from the welfare board. And he told this desperate woman that somebody would come by in the next few days to help her. Then, in a day or so, along came Dr. Cole's "bird dog."

This "Mrs. Bird-dog" is one of the strangest figures in this strange world. She is a woman who goes around finding pregnant women in Miami and telling them to go to Dr. Cole to have their baby, and she also sends couples who want to adopt children to Dr. Cole. She says she gets no money for doing this.

"Mrs. Bird-dog" told Miss Young, whose delivery was only a few weeks off, that she should go to Dr. Cole. Until Mitler, the Senate committee legal counsel, and I talked to her last week she still thought the Florida State Welfare Board had sent her to Dr. Cole.

Reflectively, Miss Young summed up her experience: "What Miami needs is more homes for girls in the trouble I was in. You can't make a law against illegitimate babies. Face it. Hundreds of girls do, and come to Miami every year to hide so their people won't know about it. They look for help and they can't find it here."

Louise Young had skirted the edge of a precipice, as I later learned when I talked to a woman who had known Dr. Cole.

"I came in Sunday after—and two hours later my sister came home. She was bleeding to death. There was nobody there that could help her. I called an ambulance, and we put my sister in the ambulance. I told the driver to take her to Jackson Hospital. I went back in the house and when I came out to follow in my car, there was this woman, this Dr. Cole. Dr. Cole and the ambulance tore off. I chased them, and we ended up at a little hospital in Coral Gables. My sister died not long after they got her there."

Police investigated Dr. Cole's claim that the dead woman had insisted on getting up and going home right after her delivery. Dr. Cole put the baby in adoption with a Miami couple.

And, with a full swing around this tragic circle, I talked last week to the woman who adopted that baby, call her Mrs. Gay.

139
▲

Mrs. Gay stood there with her well-beloved little girl in her arms and hollered at me:

"How can you do anything to hurt that good old woman? I love Dr. Cole like my own mother. She was sweet and dear and kind to me. She got this baby for me that means my life. I have known that old woman for thirty years, and she is crippled—I have always heard from childbirth. But she worked hard to raise her five kids, and if she does drive a Cadillac, she's worked a long time for it. If they ask me to go down there and testify anything about Dr. Cole, I will testify that I love her and she is wonderful.

"I'll wire Ike! How can you live with your conscience, hurting that poor old woman? I've got a pistol I'll loan you to shoot yourself with!"

Beside these women, so variously and deeply involved emotionally in this strange tangle of adopting babies, Dr Eduardo Suarez in his Naturopathic clinic at 5975 SE Eighth Street ran his business with an indifferent and commercial attitude.

"When you finally get around to trying to get a baby this way," he told me, "it's going to cost money."

The welfare board legally lets him charge $150 to deliver a girl. He wrote down that figure.

"But to have a good healthy baby you have to take care of the mother beforehand," he continued, and wrote down the figure $650. "I give the girl $20 a week to live on."

On top of that, he said, is the lawyer's fee. He looked at the two figures, thought a moment, and said that in all the amount for a baby would be a little more than $1,000.

"I'm not interested in big black market money," he remarked.

Later he said he thought the lawyer's fee was around $200.

"These girls are a big headache to me. First they want me to do an abortion, and I have to talk them out of that. I say, look, honey, you're four months pregnant. I can't abort you. Now relax, and settle down, and I'll tell you how to have this baby and I'll take care of you.

"They cry and cry and threaten suicide and try to cut themselves and need blood transfusions," he said impatiently. "The girls are expensive to take care of. The men are simpleminded. It is easy to take care of them."

He was in a hurry, and I couldn't explore the subject of why men needed taking care of in the case of illegitimate babies. He said that he didn't have a girl expecting right now, but he knew of another doctor who did. He took my New York phone number and address, and said he would call when he did find a baby for me.

"You may think I have forgotten you," he said. "It may be a long time before I call you."

He hopefully suggested that he could treat me so I could have babies. I invented a medical history that got him off that subject.

He said he was very careful not to place Philippine or Puerto Rican babies with people like me. "What you want is a baby out of a little Cracker girl," he said.

"These girls are a lot of trouble to me," he repeated. "I promised a girl $150, and she wanted more money. She called me on the phone and wanted more money, and I offered her $200. She said that was nothing compared to what she could get somewhere else. My phone might have been wiretapped and I didn't know the girl very well, so I told her 'Go someplace else, then, honey.'"

He cautioned me as I left:

"When the social workers ask you what you paid me, don't tell them. They don't like to have the girls get any help. Say it was very little, practically nothing. Say I practically gave the baby to you."

UNDERSEA SLEDDING

Looking for a cool weekend trip? How about a ride down the Gulf Stream twenty feet beneath the waves in an undersea sled? You won't forget it. If you can breathe, swim a little, and stay this side of panic, you can make the trip. The water streams past you in a cool caress. Blue is all around to infinity. There is no horizon, no bottom, only a scalloped ceiling above. You have an undersea chauffeur for company, plus some dolphins. You seem to move at terrific speed, but quite smoothly, with never a bump.

The ultimate horror of being way down under the water in the open ocean turns out to be completely beautiful. As you drag in the air from your aqualung in fast little gulps and hang on tight to the sea sled, you feel just two things in equal proportions—delight and terror.

When your chauffeur manipulates the controls of the undersea sled so that you tilt and weave from side to side, you are not slung over suddenly. The water supports you in a much kinder fashion than air does. When the sled rolls completely over and the bubbles from your breathing apparatus are streaming to the surface, you feel that the bubbles have suddenly started going down. Head down, you feel like you are right side up. The wave-scooped surface of the water seems like the bottom. The sled rights, and you are dizzy.

If you do not care to do this, you can get something of the effect from several glasses of champagne. You come out when you suddenly realize the greatest danger is that you could learn to love it under the water, want to stay. Back in the boat you are disconsolate. Air is such a sleazy product to have wrapped around your body.

We went out from Whale Harbour on Matecumbe Key with Captain

Hugh Brown in his forty-four-foot cruiser, *Reef Corsair*, for our undersea ride. Paul Arnold, president of Diving Corporation of America, and Maggy Reno, diving instructor, were to ride the undersea sled for photographs by Jerry Greenberg.

His is the toughest kind of photograph. The cameraman puts his foot through a loop in the tow rope, wraps the taut rope around his body, hangs on with one arm, and grapples with the camera in its underwater case. The cruiser towing the sled is going at very slow speed, five miles an hour, but that seems terrifically fast when you are being hauled under the water like a piece of live bait.

As the cruiser wallows slowly up the Gulf Stream, pitching through the cresting waves of the deep blue ocean, it is strange and disconcerting to watch the taut tow rope and know three people are down underneath the water out of sight at the end of the line. After the experts each used up a tank of air in photography, and that takes an hour, the time comes for the novice diver to take an undersea ride. For this exhilarating trip, you strap five pounds of lead weight around your waist and firmly hitch a tank of compressed air to your back. You put on a face mask, bite down on the mouthpiece of the aqualung to check the flow of air, then slip your feet into long swim fins.

Thus attired, you realize that the most dangerous part of the trip is the waddle across the cockpit of the pitching cruiser, because so weighted and shod you can easily fall and break your bones or spirit. You consign yourself to the forbidding waves only by pulling a complete blank and going over like a zombie.

Once you are over the side and under the water, everything changes instantly and completely. You are weightless, balanced between the buoyancy of the air tank and the lead weights. You kick with the swim fins and go back fast and easy to the sea sled, where chauffeur Arnold waits. You gulp hungrily for air, and air comes streaming into your lungs. Everywhere around you is a cool, kind, perfect blue. The water is smooth below, no matter how rough it is above. You grab the sea sled and are off on your terror-filled, beauty-filled ride.

You discover that the way fish probably communicate with each other is by the look in their eyes and the expression on their faces. Your chauffeur, perched beside you on the rods of the sled, is much magnified by the water, and you can tell instantly by every grin and grimace what he feels.

The sea sled has practical uses. Professional salvage operators find the device invaluable in locating wrecks. The Florida Game and Wildlife Service uses it for underwater surveys. The president of Venezuela has such a sled, and he reportedly uses it as your president has used the golf course—to get away from it all.

Publicity!

Marky and Steve shot a deer, and then they went back with Chisholm and found a very young fawn down in the brush, because Chisholm had noted the lower pair of eyes just before the boys shot. Mark brought it home, and I crawled in the dog house to give it a bottle. That fawn came to me, licked my cheek, and blew into my ear in the sexiest manner of any animal I ever met.

Doe Winslow came along, while I was trying to think of an appropriate name for the deer, and named him Bucky. Henry, who cut up carrots, beans, and bits of bread to his whim every evening, took up the name.

The fawn lived in Mark's bedroom for three weeks, sleeping on the foot of his bed, while Mark was building a big deer corral. Its elegant, affectionate trust of anybody who came along was enough to restore the guiltiest mortal to decent self-esteem.

At one point, before the fawn lost its spots, Mark trained it to lead him on a leash; he would slip a dog harness on the deer, and Bucky would cavort across the yard with Marky running fast behind him.

We had the Lincoln Road account at that time, and I decided to get a photo of a beautiful young blond model in Easter clothes being led by Bucky down Lincoln Road. The Easter Parade was my idea. What came out was Adrienne Boudreau taking one buck shopping on Lincoln Road.

Steve brought the deer over for the photos, keeping a sharp lookout for game wardens. The model, Adrienne, was charming.

Bucky got nervous, I fed him Coke, he spilled the Coke on Adrienne's dress, but she was really gracious. In this cavorting, we gathered a small crowd around us.

"Tell me," said a nice elderly Jewish lady, "is it a dog?"

"No lady," I said, "its a goat we got fixed up to look like a deer. It's for publicity."

"Oh," she said. "Publicity!" And her tone made my heart surge with delight that I am in this business, and no other.

BEACH WALK

For six days I walked 104 miles up the beaches of the Florida east coast, from Jupiter Light to Patrick Air Force Base. Two nights I slept on the beach, walking on between naps.

In a bag slung on one shoulder I carried cheese, raisins, and bell peppers, water in a plastic one-pint detergent bottle, a bug-bomb, a very light water-repellent jacket with hood, a plastic bag to keep my legs warm, plenty of matches, cigarettes, comb, Kleenex, a map, lipstick and enough money.

After noting on the first day that I could skinny-dip in complete privacy almost anywhere along that beach, I left my bathing suit behind to lighten the load and had no cause to regret it until the last day, when I reached a populated beach.

The idea that walking up the beach would be a good vacation came to me after the phone had rung incessantly all one day and into the evening. After studying the map, I picked that stretch because it seemed the least populated on Florida's east coast. Unpopulated it proved to be, for many, many miles.

I knew that Jonathan Dickenson, his wife, baby, and others had been ship-wrecked along there in the eighteenth century and found it so desolate that a number of their party died before they finished their walk to St. Augustine. But they walked hungry, naked, in the winter, and were prisoners of hostile Indians.

I picked the first week in May, and on the nights I did not sleep on the beach, I called my daughter-in-law, Vera, who lives in Stuart. She came and picked me up, fed me a good dinner, and I slept comfortably in her house.

The thing I learned was faith.

Have faith that walking is a means of getting somewhere, and the blue headlands before you will fade into the blue distance behind you.

If, upon walking on the second day, you totter along the sand with new muscles in your legs and feet complaining, put one foot in front of the other for three minutes and the kinks and pains will go, and you can step out happily. The same thing holds true with a cramp in the calf of the leg in mid-afternoon.

Have faith that you can walk twenty miles on a pint of water, and you will find you can, especially if the water tastes slightly of detergent. This will deter you from wanting too much water.

The same dense, beautiful, and inpenetrable green that was so forbidding to Jonathan Dickenson mantles the rolling dune behind the beach today for many miles. Sea grapes, palmettos, and coco plum are woven together into a wall. Only the shore birds that were laying pink eggs, raccoons, and a little animal that left tiny tracks and wedge-shaped holes in the sand seemed to find the underbrush hospitable.

The little tracks proved to be those of armadillos; they like to stick their noses in the sand now and then. There were no signs of the small bears that used to come down to Jupiter Beach to eat turtle eggs when Captain Bill Gray and his brother Herman camped out there in 1909.

That coast is fringed by long, narrow islands, and it was on the beaches of those islands I walked. There is no bridge across the St. Lucie Inlet at the northern tip of Jupiter Island, the first stretch of my journey. I should have had to backtrack eight miles or so had a fisherman not ferried me across that inlet to the southern tip of Hutchinson Island.

To me the Stuart House of Refuge, about two miles north of St. Lucie's inlet, was just that. Built in the 1880s to afford succor to shipwrecked sailors who might otherwise have perished from hunger and thirst on that desolate coast, it is today maintained as a fascinating little museum by the local historical society, and I rested there luxuriously. Just off shore treasure hunters were working.

A road is being built the length of Hutchinson Island, but it is not yet completed, and access to the beach for many miles north of Jensen's Beach is only possible by foot or by beach buggy. That shimmering, firm, level strand was populated mostly by birds. There is no bridge across Ft. Pierce Inlet, at the northern tip of this island, and I went back to the mainland there across the Ft. Pierce causeway.

The third island, which I was told is also called Hutchinson Island, is about thirty miles long. My map showed no road north of Wabasso Beach, and no bridge over Sebastian Inlet. Just at dawn I rounded the northern tip of that island, and there was the most beautiful new bridge arching over Sebastian Inlet. Later I found it was opened in February. That was when I really pondered on the message: Have faith.

For six days I walked when I wanted to walk, ate when I wanted to eat, and slept when and where I wanted to sleep. In the nights when I got sleepy, I combed the eroding sandy bluff to a casuarina tree, scraped up some needles and small dead twigs and branches, and started a little fire.

After my feet were warm, I put out the fire and raked the hot sand out to make a bed. My bag was my pillow, and I wiggled out curves in the sand to fit. Never did I have a sounder, sweeter sleep—even though I usually waked chilly in two or three hours. The chill went away when I walked. The nights were most magical after the moon had set, for the stars were higher and so lavish in their brightness that I could see the white crests of all the curling waves.

At the end, I backtracked, and my walk ended in a little white board building overlooking a splendid beach opposite Melbourne Beach trailer village. The sign says simply, "The Bar." For six days I had talked to almost no strangers. I plodded in and over my beer visited with the bartenders, Janie and Jamie.

I told them what I had been doing. Jamie came from behind the bar and put soothing drops in my eyes and rubbed my ankles. Bob Jacobs, a customer, sent across the street to the trailer village for an electric vibrating machine, unplugged the juke box, and massaged my legs. Nobody would let me buy a beer.

So...it might be that some day I shall be drowned by the sea, or die of pneumonia from sleeping out at night, or be robbed and strangled by strangers. These things happen. Even so, I shall be ahead because of trusting the beach, the night, and strangers.

JUST CALL ME MUD

"It wasn't easy, but I got her.

"She is a constant joy and revelation. She lives with nature, close to
earth, is unpretentious. Jane doesn't
have time for mundane things. A
sense of great balance and great
beauty is demonst

and in her life. T
tion, no vanity.
soul and spirit.

"She's a nor
needs editing,
walls of Madison
it. And staying
tion she shows
Doesn't preach
always involved
shoes off anywh

"Some peo
Jane. They ar
who feed the
rarely read a
Their closed
They have no
their opposi
beautiful per

▲ Just Call Me Mud: A Biography of Jane Wood Reno ▼

She was born Jane Wallace Wood on May 28, 1913, in Macon, Georgia. Her father, George Washington Wood, Jr., had grown up on a small farm with, according to his Aunt Lil, "his mind on Milton and his eyes on Greece and Rome." Despite the disadvantages of his youth, he graduated from Mercer University at the age of eighteen, went on to Mercer Law School, and opened a practice in Macon. Jane's mother, Daisy Sloan Hunter Wood, was from Mecklenberg County, North Carolina, part of a heritage that went back to Henry Hunter and the Mecklenberg Declaration. Married in 1910, the couple had five children in eight years—Jane, Do... Winifred, and Geo... Jane, the oldes... lished herself early... leader and adventurer... her siblings, but her... instilled a strong sense o... and family in all the chil... Jane's sister Daisy becam... nurse in World War II a... served in North Africa wit... General Patton's army. She married Phil Winslow and brought up a family in the Florida Keys. Dolly married Bill Denslow and raised two children on North Kendall Drive, the same road in Miami where Jane lived with her family. George went to medical school, set up a practice in Bangor, Maine, and raised a large family with h... wife, Adelle Sawyer...

Her pride and joy was the chimney, made of
soft, orange brick. She bought the bricks for ten ce
apiece from the owner of a burned-down house, pi
ing them out of the rubble and cleaning them one a
time. Helped along by federal pamphlets on "How
build a fireplace," she carefully designed it so that
would draw properly. The only time it failed to do
was the Christmas a peacock fell down it into a roari
fire.

The house was finished in late October 1951, at
total cost of $7217.39. In the course of constructing i
she and Henry had changed the plans from a two-stor
to a one-story house with two big bedrooms, a kitche
with a fireplace, and the large red-brick porch. In th
following years, they added an east wing consisting o
two more bedrooms divided from the main house by
breezeway. By the time she finished the house, Jane
had added a new wealth of skills to a mind and body
not easily daunted.

"I found this: You can learn or do anything you
want, if you aren't hurried."

▲   Photo on previous spread: Writing, as always. This picture was taken at Jane's
family home in 1933, when she was twenty years old.

When National Airlines began their Miami-London service, Jane Wood Reno suggested to the mayor of Miami Beach that it might be a great gesture of goodwill to send the mayor of London an alligator for the London Zoo. Jane even offered to supply the alligator. She went out to her Miccosukee friends in the Everglades and got a small gator from them, quickly taped up its jaws, and brought it home.

While the alligator sulked resentfully on the Reno porch in the hours before the trip to the airport, the tape came loose. Jane quickly grabbed another roll of tape and prepared to secure its mouth again, but the creature had other ideas. It snapped off a piece of her fingertip, and almost got her hand. She later recalled:

"I wasn't fast enough, I hesitated—I forgot what I used to preach about being quick and smooth. I stopped for just an instant when I had my fingers under his jaws and was coming around to clamp the top of his snout. He jerked his head sideways and chomped off the end of my finger."

Blood poured out of the finger. Jane's daughter-in-law Vera helped her pen the alligator away in the fireplace behind a make-shift fence, and they rushed for the emergency room. They left a sign scrawled on the door:

"DANGER: Bad Alligator"

The family doctor, long used to the bizarre injuries of the perennially active Renos, sighed and said to the emergency room nurses:

"You probably won't treat many grandmothers with alligator bites."

The damage turned out to be much less serious than it had looked. With her finger stitched up, Jane went home, started taping up the alligator's jaws all over again, and finally got the creature safely off to London.

Jane Wood Reno never contented herself with the conventional. She was a spirited pioneer who slogged through Everglades muck, posed as a wealthy woman wishing to buy a baby, trekked around Greece, built a house for her family with her own hands, and championed the Seminole Indians.

She was born Jane Wallace Wood on May 28, 1913, in Macon, Georgia. Her father, George Washington Wood, Jr., had grown up on a small farm with, according to his Aunt Lil, "his mind on Milton and his eyes on Greece and Rome." Despite the disadvantages of his youth, he graduated from Mercer University at the age of eighteen, went on to Mercer Law School, and opened a practice in Macon. Jane's mother, Daisy Sloan Hunter Wood, was from Mecklenburg County, North Carolina, part of a heritage that went back to Henry Hunter and the Mecklenburg Declaration. Married in 1910, the couple had five children in eight years—Jane, Dolly, Daisy, Winifred, and George.

Jane, the oldest, established herself early as the leader and adventurer among her siblings, but her mother instilled a strong sense of duty and family in all the children. Jane's sister Daisy became a nurse in World War II and served in North Africa with General Patton's army. She married Phil Winslow and brought up a family in the Florida Keys. Dolly married Bill Denslow and raised two children on North Kendall Drive, the same road in Miami where Jane lived with her family. George went to medical school, set up a practice in Bangor, Maine, and raised a large family with his wife, Adelle Sawyer Wood.

Winifred, the youngest of the Wood children, shared much of Jane's fierce individuality and confidence. During World War II, Winifred joined the WASPs, the Women's Air Force Service Pilots, the first organized group of female flyers to serve their country. They trained male pilots, towed targets, ferried Air Force planes to different bases around the country, and tested B-25s, B-17s, and other combat aircraft. The WASPs were quite a shock to the male world of the Air Force, and it took a lot of staying power to withstand the knocks that came with the territory. She chronicled the adventures of this spirited group of women in her book *We Were WASPS*, and today shares a house in the San Bernardino mountains with a WASP comrade and the artist for her book, Dorothy Swain Lewis.

Jane and her siblings grew up at 107 Courtland Avenue in Macon and spent their summers in Sunnyside, at the Georgia farmhouse built by their father's father. The story is told that Jane's grandfather, George Washington Wood, came up the railway line from Americus until he found a town that didn't have a general store. Besides running the general store and post office, he served as station master and made the rounds of the countryside as a Baptist preacher. Because the Baptist Church didn't have a burying ground in Sunnyside, his tombstone is at the Methodist Church, and it reads:

"For twenty-seven years pastor of country churches in middle Georgia. He preached Jesus."

The house in Sunnyside was a gathering place for generations of family members during Jane's lifetime. In the final months of her life, after countless joyous times in countless joyous places, it was Sunnyside that she reminisced about most often. Her sister Winifred remembers from her childhood:

"Grandmother made marvelous large rolls for Sunday morning breakfast which we had with syrup and fresh milk. She did the cooking for all those people all those summers plus working in the garden, hoeing, killing chickens by wringing their necks, milking the cow, churning, and I couldn't begin to guess what else. Some lady!"

By the time Jane was six years old, she knew she wanted to write. For many years she saved a page from her first writing book which read "Jane Wallace Wood: Author." When she was a fourth-grader at Winship Elementary in Macon, her teachers recommended that she skip a grade. At first, her parents thought it might be a bad idea to push her too hard, but field consultants from the National Committee for Mental Hygiene came to Macon around this time to establish a child guidance clinic. Her parents agreed to send Jane there for testing. A battery of tests revealed an IQ of 167. Her early notoriety as a genius and the troubles it caused became the subject of one of her favorite stories:

"There was a story in the *Macon Daily Telegraph* with a headline I remember: 'Jane Wood Declared Genius.' It said I had the highest IQ in Georgia. I found out something. I found out there was nothing like being declared a genius to make people hate you. I had to go out and fight all of the boys on the block to prove I was still me."

She completed the work of the seventh grade in two months and began high school at the age of eleven, the youngest student at the Lanier High School for Girls. She played on the freshman basketball team and pursued swimming, baseball, tennis, and horseback riding as well. For a hobby she collected stamps. An article about Jane in the *Macon Daily Telegraph* of December 14, 1924, had the following to say about her:

> Dickens, Scott, Kipling, history, all are old friends of Jane's. She likes boys' stories and stories of adventure and animal stories. She loves nature and studies it. On a recent trip through Florida, one of her teachers, who was a member of the party, says Jane failed to name only two of the birds they saw, and, not only knew the names of all of the others, but their habits as well.
>
> Miss Falk...says that she has examined literally thousands of children and that Jane is one of the most brilliant, if not the most brilliant, she had ever passed on. Dr. Robinson made practically the same remark, and his examinations have been made all over the United States.
>
> But one of the outstanding features in the case of Jane Wood is that despite her brilliance of mind, her natural ability to read, the unanimous praise constantly accorded her work and mentality, she remains an unassuming, simple child, loving best of everything in the whole wide world her father and mother, her sisters and brother—and her home, separation from which, for even a short period of time, means loss of appetite, loss of interest, and a life left bare of everything but one—a desire to return home.

157
▲

The love that she found and gave at home was central to Jane Wood's life. To her, home was not an address, but any place in which her extended family gathered and put down roots. Throughout her youth, Sunnyside was as much that home as Macon, and she provided her family with a Florida equivalent to Sunnyside when she built her house in Miami in 1949.

In 1925, Jane's father, attracted by the booming growth of Florida, moved his family from Macon to Miami. Jane was disappointed with her new environment until the hurricane of 1926, an exciting event which she later saw as the beginning of her love affair with Florida. Tragically, the hurricane marked the beginning of Miami's collapse and the long years of the Great Depression to follow, but Jane nevertheless immersed herself in activity with her usual infectious enthusiasm. She inadvertently skipped another grade when she told Miami High administrators that she was a sophomore.

Two years after the hurricane, she was associate editor at the Miami High School *Stingaree*, and she wrote about high school sports for the *Miami News*. In some notes from this time, she recalled:

"In 1928, I read in the *Saturday Evening Post* a story by Marjorie Stoneman Douglas, entitled 'Beautiful and Beloved.' It was an account of the 1926 hurricane in Miami that was just like my experience, an account of falling in love because of the force, the strength of it all. I asked our boss, journalism teacher Amanda Louise Falkner, if I could interview Marjorie Douglas. She said I could, and I called Marjorie, and she also said I could.

"She was the first person I ever interviewed. My pencil point broke when I was taking notes, probably because my hand trembled so. I asked Marjorie about her story about the storm. 'That wasn't my story,' she replied, 'that was Mabel Dorn's. I wasn't here then, I was out of town at the time.'"

Nevertheless, the interview experience was a revelation for the young journalist. Through pioneering Miami writers like Marjorie Douglas and Mabel Dorn, Jane discovered the joy of collecting stories and passing them on to wider audiences.

Finishing high school at fifteen, Jane enrolled at the University of Miami. She began as an English major, but she didn't always concentrate on her classes. There were many other things for the university's youngest student to do. One day during her sophomore year, a newspaper hit the stands with the headline "Four Miami U. Girls Missing; Foul Play Feared."

"We were sitting in a car, four of us with nothing to do. The other three were flunking college and they decided to run away. Heck, it was just a lark, something to do. I said, 'I'm going too.' I wasn't flunking, but I was damned if I was going to be left out."

They hitchhiked north, spending a night on the road before they got to Ocala. They didn't want their parents to worry, so two of the girls wired home: "Am married, going north." Jane wired:

"Jane Beatwick and Agnes married, going north, back tomorrow, don't worry, love, Jane."

From Ocala, one of them called a friend, and Jane's father came up and brought them all back home. While the others faced disapproval from their families, Jane's father asked only, "Are you okay, honey?"

Any infamy she might have faced after this ill-fated incident still did not dampen her adventurous spirit. Her proudest accomplishment in her early college years was learning to hold down five home brews before lunch, at a time when Prohibition had made drinking a grand adventure.

After her first two years at the University of Miami, diversions began to crowd out scholarly pursuits, and Jane failed both journalism and physical education, disciplines in which she was unquestionably skilled. She put her college education on hold and went out to get an education in the world, moving to Greece to live with her Aunt Peg and Uncle Bal. Peg was her mother's little sister, Margaret Sloan Hunter, and Bal was Dr. Marshall Balfour, a pioneer in world public health who worked first on malaria control in Greece and later with the Population Council in India and the Far East.

Jane taught English classes, hiked the Greek Isles, and immersed herself in the cultures of Greece and Persia. Later in life she would share her discoveries with her grandchildren, revisiting this part of the world with them and hunting down the grave of the fourteenth-century Persian poet Hafiz. She was fond of quoting his lines:

> When you hear the words of the high in heart
> Don't say that they are wrong
> It is you who do not understand the words, my friend....

159
▲

When Jane returned from Greece in 1932, Miami was in the depths of the depression. She went back to the university, this time without the home brew, and switched her major to physics:

"I asked what the science closest to metaphysics was and they said physics. I knew I could learn a lot of things from reading. I wanted to get into something I had to learn in the laboratory. I learned a little about what makes things work. I got so people couldn't put something over on me with a lot of scientific talk. I got straight A's in physics and math, and I flunked journalism."

After she graduated, she got a job as a social worker, which she describes in her story "The Best We Could." She was considering going back to school to get a Masters in social work at Columbia, but abandoned the idea after the 1935 hurricane. When she was unable to stomach the pathetic failure of social workers to provide relief from that disaster, she went back to writing and got a full-time job at the *Miami Herald*. There she met Henry Olaf Reno, a Danish immigrant who had been working as a police reporter at the *Herald* since the year Jane came to Florida.

Henry's family immigrated to the United States in 1910 when he was nine years old, the same year Jane's parents were married. They settled in Wisconsin, moved to Bartow, Florida, three years later, then to Tennessee, where Henry attended the University of Tennessee for two years, majoring in agriculture. They finally settled down for good in Miami in 1923. Henry's father had changed their name to Reno while they were still in Denmark, in anticipation of coming to America. Robert Marius Rasmussen took a random stab at a map of the U.S., hit on the city of Reno, Nevada, and decided that it was as good a name as any for his family. Because he had been a photographer in Denmark, Robert M. Reno became a photographer with the *Miami Herald*.

Henry's father helped Henry get the job at the *Herald* as police reporter, which he was to keep for the next forty-one years. The police came to trust Henry and regarded him as the best police reporter in town. Ironically, the only person ever to beat him to a story was his wife. Jane had talked to him about a case involving a policeman as the inside man for a hold-up gang. Henry had offered his help, suggesting she talk to Police Chief Walter Headley. When she showed up in Headley's office to cover the case, he asked her:

"But what about Henry?"

"He's off today," she responded.

Jane scooped everyone, including her husband, on the story, and she received "The Big Story" award for her article. Henry was amused rather than embarrassed at being outdone by his successful wife.

Among rewrite men, Henry's reporting was legendary, both for the enormous amount of information he compacted into his telephone calls, and for the eloquence and gentleness of his storytelling. His reports were often unpleasant, like this one that Jane recounted in 1979 for an article in the *Miami Herald's Tropic Magazine*:

"...Then here comes the husband home from work, you see, never suspecting. He opens the door, and what does he find? His wife's body on the living room floor and blood all over. She's been stabbed seventeen times. (That's from homicide.) He goes into the kitchen and there's the man's body. He's still holding the gun he used to shoot himself."

Yet with the way that Henry told such a story, she said, it could have been a fairy tale.

The story of how Jane and Henry became engaged was also recounted in the *Tropic Magazine* article of 1979:

> Jane was about to go back to college, to Columbia, when Henry Reno happened to mention at The Herald that crawfishing season was opening the next day; he was going to spend his day off in the Keys to fill a sack.
>
> "Take me, take me," cried Jane.
>
> "You know how to catch a crawfish?"
>
> "Sure."
>
> Henry's was a lovable gullibility.
>
> "Pick me up in front of the Coral Gables Theater," Jane said, not wanting him lost looking for her house in the Gables. She was waiting at dawn, sitting on the curb.
>
> Henry had a boat and some Cobb's Creek whiskey for curing a diver's shivers. He'd go over the side for crawfish and come aboard to warm up. "Here's to the Argentine Navy," he'd holler, toasting the rolling ocean. Jane hung on a long time but then got sick. Passed out. It's a bold, broad step from home-brew to Cobb's Creek, taken neat atop the waves.
>
> Henry took care of everything. His parents were away, so he took her to his house, carried her in and put her to bed. He put an ice pack on her head. When she woke up it was evening. *The Blue Danube* was playing, fresh crawfish and melted butter awaited her hunger. And Henry, all unsuspecting, had taken on a fateful glow.
>
> "I was afraid that would be the end of it. I didn't think he'd ever ask me anywhere again. But he did."
>
> In fact, it wasn't long after that, holding her hands, he proposed. Or Jane thought he did, so she accepted. Going over it afterward she thought, "God, was that what he really said?" She let it stand though. After they were married, she brought it up. He hemmed, "Aw," and said finally, "I guess I could have gotten out of it—if I'd wanted to."

They were married on July 20, 1937, and the couple settled into a house in Coconut Grove. Exactly one year and one day later, Jane Wood Reno gave birth to Janet. During the next four years, they had Robert Marius (named after Henry's father), Margaret Sloan (after Jane's grandmother and aunt), and Mark Wood Reno. They moved farther away from the city, to South Miami, where Henry could fulfill his aspirations toward farm life. The family had goats, a chicken, and a cow, and during World War II they sold fryers and butter.

Jane raised chickens, turkeys, and bees, and before long they bought twenty-one acres on North Kendall Drive for five hundred dollars an acre, so they could have more goats and another cow. They lived in a small yellow house at the front of the property, in an area that was way out in the country at the time. There was nothing between them and the Everglades but a barren landscape of scrub, the occasional pine, and a lot of rock.

The property was a veritable menagerie. Peacocks, squirrels, goats, chickens, cows, dogs, and ponies made the Kendall area their home, and the children brought home an endless procession of pets for temporary and sometimes long-term stays. Although she enjoyed the wealth of animals, Jane could never accept the ubiquitous mice that even the indigo snake couldn't control. One night she shook Henry awake to tell him a mouse had run across the bottom of the bed.

"You gotta hand it to 'em!" he said, and went promptly back to sleep.

It was during this time, in the late 1940s, that the Reno family began a seemingly neverending series of adventures. They almost always end up stuck in the mud, or with everyone sopping wet, or both. Perhaps the first was a trip down to Flamingo in 1947, when there was no national park and the road was greasy grey muck. Jane showed the children how to catch a raccoon, how to get stuck, and how to get unstuck. Later that year Jane and Henry borrowed a horse van, put bunk beds in it, and spent three weeks discovering Florida.

On a trip to the Smokies, they stayed in a hundred-year-old log cabin with a cookhouse that a hungry bear kept ransacking. When Jane asked the ranger's wife what they should do about the bear, the woman replied, "Shoot it, honey," and loaned her a shotgun. Henry held the light when the bear came by for its nightly raid, and Jane dispatched the unfortunate creature.

One day in 1949, a strange man covered in mud walked into the driveway of the little yellow house. With his odd way of talking that Jane would come to love, he announced that his swamp buggy was stuck and introduced himself as "Sippi" Morris. He seemed to be curious about these people who had a jeep and lived so far out on Kendall Drive. Remarkably enough, he could talk longer and faster than Jane, and he never ran out of stories. Sippi revealed to her the mysteries of the wild and wonderful swamp known as the Everglades, taught her how to wrestle alligators, and introduced her to the Seminoles. The Reno children fondly remember him as a great storyteller who came and went randomly for forty years, always a welcome surprise.

Despite the years of adventure spent there, the little yellow house no longer seemed large enough for the Wood family. Jane decided to design her ideal home. She wanted space to accommodate the whole family and visitors, and a wide open design fronted by a screened-in porch half the size of the entire house. Life, in her opinion, was not meant to be lived in closed-off rooms; the spacious porch was to become a gathering place for generations of people from every walk of life.

When Jane went out in the summer of 1949, bought a pick at the local hardware store, and began chipping away at the limestone on the "east ten," Henry didn't quite know what to make of it. When it became clear that she was planning to build a new house, he sold enough acreage for her to be able to afford materials and helped her on his days off. After having the plans made up in June 1949, Jane spent months and months of arduous work breaking through the rock. The children's mumps, PTA meetings, and Christmas festivities slowed the work, but by March of 1950 the foundation was ready to pour.

Just as Sippi became her genius of the swamps, A. Travers Ewell became the genius of the house. This engineer and adventurer with the bristling white mustache also had an inexhaustible supply of stories. He and his wife Peggy ran the adobe brick company where Jane purchased her bricks, and he advised her on a range of structural matters. He was also the leader of the South Miami Cub Scout pack, of which she became a den mother.

Jane learned the building trades as she went along. Every time she came upon an unfamiliar task, she would visit building sites to pick the brains of workers or hire someone for however long it took to learn their skills, usually a day. In an accounts ledger, she kept track of the costs in meticulous detail. One entry notes an expense of $1.80 for nine beers for the plumber. Her son Mark recalls:

"The plumber was an old drunk that H. O. (Henry) found down at the Spotlight Bar. Didn't even do the job right. We had to fix up the mess he made."

After receiving the building permit in March, Jane worked steadily

163
▲

throughout the rest of the year, and by Christmas of 1950 she had finished much of the base of the house, including the porch, part of the chimney, the plumbing, and much of the adobe walls. When funds ran low, she would write an article for the *Miami News Sunday Magazine*.

"I'd write a story and get twenty-five dollars for it, then I'd buy more block for the house."

After the holidays were over, she took on the house with renewed enthusiasm. By the end of January she'd finished much of the house's wood frame, which consisted of sturdy cypress posts and tie-beams. At this point, Henry said, "By damn, she really is building a house," and he took two weeks off to put up the roof beams with the help of his ninety-year-old father. Working relentlessly through the spring, she had the roof on and shingled by early summer. The cedar shingles were planed to such exact specifications, and nailed on by her so precisely that a felt underlayer wasn't necessary.

The original roof came unscathed through Hurricane Donna in the 1960s, and the shingles have been replaced by family members in twenty year cycles, a task passed on from generation to generation. Each time the shingles are put on exactly the way they were done originally, a job that would cost $25,000 today if done by a contractor. In 1951 she did it herself for a little over five hundred dollars.

Her pride and joy was the chimney, made of old, soft, orange brick. She bought the bricks for ten cents apiece from the owner of a burned-down house, picking them out of the rubble and cleaning them one at a time. Helped along by federal pamphlets on "How to build a fireplace," she carefully designed it so that it would draw properly. The only time it failed to do so was the Christmas a peacock fell down it into a roaring fire.

The house was finished in late October 1951, at a total cost of $7217.39. In the course of constructing it, she and Henry had changed the plans from a two-story to a one-story house with two big bedrooms, a kitchen with a fireplace, and the large red-brick porch. In the following years, they added an east wing consisting of two more bedrooms divided from the main house by a breezeway. By the time she finished the house, Jane had added a new wealth of skills to a mind and body not easily daunted.

"I found this: You can learn or do anything you want, if you aren't hurried."

Jane didn't let raising four children and building a house stand in the way of other pursuits. She won her first Big Story award in 1950, for a pair of articles she wrote for the *Miami Herald* in 1949 on a strange sickness afflicting

Seminole Indian children. ("The Big Story" was a national radio-TV program sponsored by Pall Mall that broadcast renditions of the best stories in journalism.) In fact, it was during the time she was building the house that her lifelong friendship with the Seminoles and the Everglades began.

Throughout the 1950s, she took her newspaper career to great heights for someone who had flunked journalism in college. Each new assignment brought her more acclaim, and her talent and increased output resulted in a curious situation at the *Miami News*. Because the paper didn't want it to appear that the same journalist wrote too many of its articles, she often wrote under other names, alternately using Jane Wood, Richard Wallace, John H. Reynolds, and Don Renold. In 1955, she scooped Henry on the police story and won the Big Story award again.

During these years, she learned to wrestle small alligators with the Seminoles, explored springs and rivers, took part in the pioneering of scuba diving in Florida, led a cub scout pack and raced scooters victoriously in Cub Scout Den Mother races, and generally kept as busy as humanly possible.

One of her favorite getaway places with the family was Plantation Key, where Travers and Peggy Ewell owned a house with a porch just like hers. They snorkeled on the reefs, beachcombed the rocky shore, and marveled at the virginity of it all. One day Jane sailed the little dinghy out to sea to reach the light at Hens and Chickens reef, leaving a worried band of children ashore when she sailed out of sight. She tacked her way back, still exultant at the sense of going, and quoted Kipling:

> *We must go-go-go away from here!*
> *On the side the world we're overdue*
> *'Send your road is clear before you when the old Spring*
> *fret comes o'er you*
> *And the red Gods call for you."*

The house and property became more of a menagerie than ever, as Jane's daughter Maggy remembers:

"Daddy would come out of the bathroom and and say 'Would somebody come get this'—and you can interject pelican, otter, boa constrictor—'out of here so I can take a bath?'"

The following letter Jane wrote to her sister Winifred—affectionately known as Reddy—in 1957 gives insight into her life during the late fifties. Because she loved Winifred dearly, conflicts with her youngest sister could be especially caustic, fueled by their strong-minded and opinionated

165
▲

natures. Maggy Reno Hurchalla remembers the prospective visit mentioned in the letter as "perhaps being the time when Mother hit Winnie with an ironing board." Jane's deeply felt love for both her family and her work is obvious in the following letter.

Dearest Reddy,

The days are getting long, the wonderful rose and gold clouds are piling up in summer sunsets, and all about me is that delicious feeling that has come to signal summer: They are coming home! Janet and Mark and You. My chillun go away and come again most in summer, even ere now, so it has come to have that exciting feeling in it that used to be in Christmas. Aunt Peg and Aunt Nell are also coming.

Janet will leave Cornell June 11th and come home by bus, perhaps stopping for a night and a day with Nina Balfour in Washington to see Washington. Markie will leave Bangor shortly after June 15th, by bus, and also perhaps stop over at Nina's. They decided regretfully in Bangor that Mark's 1948 Ford couldn't possibly make the trip, so he is going to sell it, for about $75 I gather. You will probably be glad not to ride with them in $75 worth of Ford. I sure as God would be. Aunt Peg and Aunt Nell are coming down around the first of June for a visit, staying at Uncle Parks. It ought to be a right wonderful summer.

Janet has a job in the City of Miami communications promised, $60 a week. She also has a job for Cornell next year that will pay her the equivalent of $960 in room and board, so we are right proud of her. In her chemistry pre-lim, she made the highest mark in the class, 95, and the class average was 65. She adores Cornell, and has had some indication that Cornell loves Janny Baby.

Bob has registered at Tulane, which should be quite perfect for him. He had rather hoped for one of the Eastern colleges to which he applied, but his grade average C blocked his admission there. It is very tough the last two or three years, and from now on indefinitely, to get admitted to good colleges. There are about seven applications for every opening. However Tulane is good and more solid scholastically than the University of North Carolina, which might have otherwise been his choice. New Orleans will be a wonderful city for him, too, he and I both think. He is quite happy. He is having a fine time winding up high school with proms and banquets. You never saw a smarter 17 year old in a tuxedo than my six foot three inch Bob. He is still headed for the law, in a totally relaxed sort of way.

Maggy is reaping honors in school with an even slightly wider swath than Janet. As of now she will be valedictorian next year, though that could change. She has won the Biology medal and the History medal and the county United Nations $50 contest prize, and some debate honors. She has a literary style I consider gifted and is a fine mathematician. She is also six feet one inch tall and a raving beauty, and reminds me more of you when she wakes up in the morning than anybody I ever knew. Sunny disposition otherwise. She plans to spend the summer teaching aqua-lung diving as a teacher for Diving Corp. of America.

Mark I am very homesick for. He has had a wonderful time in Bangor, been sweet and helpful and loving, they say, at the George Woods, and dotes on them. He was on the Bangor High football team, right tackle. Does lousy school work, can't read worth a damn. He is 6 feet 4, weighs 190, is the most gorgeous hunk of young man you ever saw and has all the emotional maturity of a little yellow duck.

I have missed him and Janet so this winter—much too quiet and peaceful without them.

We enjoyed George's and Delle's visit so. They are a perfectly wonderful family, nicer than ever. Being with them is like being rocked on a broad, peaceful sea of love. None of the eight of them criticize each other or other people. Delle is beginning to look mildly haggard, like me. The youngest, their Janny baby, is a beauty. They are all such lovely children they make me yearn for grandchildren. Floyd and Sally Winslow are very dear children, too. Doe is a plump, shrieking beauty who will be so when she outgrows the shrieking.

Mother and Daddy enjoyed it all, but it was an impact on them because Daisy ended by staying with them. Your mother is getting old, and deafer, and needs a lot of gentleness. There is a little bit of heart-wrenching fragility about her, and a slight plaintive quality of real age. I think it comes in part from the deafness, because you have to speak louder, and when people have to speak louder we don't always remember to speak as gently. To see her age is more lacerating than I can bear to think about. She is looking forward to your visit with great pleasure. When you come home this time, don't act as though the fact that we regret you live away from us is a reproach. Nobody means to reproach you, or net you here to us. You have that kind of wary feeling, as though we were clinging, or covertly blaming you for something, that you go again, perhaps. Actually, Mother and Daddy and I don't feel that way. We have become people of the world, the world is our home. Missing you and loving you dearly is something different from reproach or trying to tie you down.

I am enjoying my newspapering pretty good right now. I had to regretfully give up working for Hank Meyer for awhile—too crushing a load. But Hank is darling. We have been having some fine lively issues and events and cases this winter for the Special Report I write three or four times a week. I am certainly the best known and best newspaper woman in Florida, having become twice blasted in the current session of the legislature. (Blasted by villains whose displeasure it is an honor to incur.) The nice thing about my job is that there is in one way no ceiling to it. I can tackle the big, the complex, the difficult and the hot stories, and be so controversial I move from hot water to warm to boiling, with the blessings of my bosses.

The challenge is to grasp and to communicate, fairly and accurately, in the most important local issues. For example: second mortgage racketeering and regulation, small loan shenanigans, the case of the brain-washed grand juries, the Seminole peace treaty (proposed), the U.S. Army Engineers flood control policies, hurricane research, a great feud over the Jackson Psychiatric Institute, the Puerto Rican farm labor camps. These are issues on which there have been a number of widely separated viewpoints in recent months. They take a degree of research, leg-work. They are complex, and must be presented lucidly and vividly, but without over-simplification or distortion. I write something that is like a short magazine article, but it is specific, pin-pointed and local. I don't do a column, it is not that rigid or personalized. But it has a lot wider range of subject and of personalizing permitted than the regular reporter.

This feature has sort of evolved in the last two years, and is cherished fairly highly by my bosses as well as by me, and is peculiarly congenial. It would be hard to go stale on, since it is always new and varying and demanding, and since I have a fair control in the tacks and tangents I can go off on. You can't coast on it, either, or get stupid. Last month I went to Gainesville for a two-day seminar on nuclear energy, consorting with a lovely bunch of scientists, and last week out into the Everglades to sit in on a Seminole council meeting where I am the only reporter in the world really welcomed. (Probably because I am the only reporter in the world that will bother to go to most all of the important council meetings and be extremely careful to get it all accurately.) One real beauty about this particular thing, in case you think I sound stuffy and vainglorious is that I get a good deal of hammering in return on some of these things, and am subject to plenty of acid criticism within and outside of my office—things that begin with, "You and your goddamn vain hyperthyroid, look what you did now..." It's a lot of fun, and I wouldn't be doing anything else though I wish I could make twice as much money.

Looking deeply into the workings and life of a big city is a very fascinating way to spend your time. Miami is very exciting to me, a true metropolis, an adequate education. I have developed a feeling for it of the type and magnitude that some of the really great city lovers have had for the really great cities—like Proust had for Paris, say. Miami with a ring of mountains could be, to me, the world's greatest city, always with a few hundred thousand things about it to clean, straighten, polish, or erase. You can curse it so, too—there is nothing piddling about its flaws. My current long-time crusade is against a poisonous and insidious paranoid conformity and malicious and vicious pseudo-reforming: i.e., I am crusading against crusades. You can't believe how this subtle corrosive has eaten into the old go-to-hell and tolerant town you grew up in. I hope to see the day we turn back toward the mean that lies somewhere between the old free and easy wide open Miami and now.

Flit home as quick as you can, we'll have a wonderful time.

Love,
Jane

With Janet at Cornell, Robert at Tulane, and Maggy set to enter college at Swarthmore, Jane and Henry sold more of the property to finance their children's educations. Jane was at the peak of her career as a journalist, while at the same time doing what was essentially public relations work for the Seminoles in their struggles to reclaim their land. Between that and the work she had done for Hank Meyer, her flair for public relations work had become obvious. She had always loved drama, and public relations work was the perfect stage for showing off. The costs of keeping three children in college were beyond the means of a pair of reporters, even ones as frugal as Henry and Jane. For these reasons and others, the temptation of a better-paying career became great for Jane.

Hints from her boss at the *Miami News*, Bill Baggs, that she might be taken off her Special Report feature and assigned to a duller beat infuriated her. The Special Report feature was her pride and joy, and she had done as much as anyone to make it successful. If the *News* would let her go, she told Hank Meyer, she would go to work for him. In a story in the July 1969 issue of the *Village Post*, Hank Meyer recalled steeling himself and dialing a number one day.

"Uncle Dan," he said, "I have a favor to ask. I want to hire one of your people."

Dan Mahoney was the editor of the *Miami News,* and he was one of the people at the paper that Jane adored. When Hank Meyer told him that he wanted to hire Mahoney's star reporter away from him, a less-than-friendly exchange of remarks took place.

"You want her that much?" Mahoney said, after calming down. "She's one of the best we have. It hurts."

In a *Village Post* article of 1967, Meyer remembered:

"It wasn't easy, but I got her.

"She is a constant joy and revelation. She lives with nature, close to earth, is unpretentious. Jane doesn't have time for mundane things. A sense of great balance and great beauty is demonstrated in her work and in her life. There is no frustration, no vanity. Her makeup is her soul and spirit.

"She's a nonconformist, never needs editing, can tear down the walls of Madison Avenue. Such spirit. And staying power. In any situation she shows excellent judgment. Doesn't preach. No crusades, but always involved. And she takes her shoes off anywhere.

"Some people don't understand Jane. They are the kind of people who feed their bodies with food, rarely read a book, early to bed. Their closed minds sap their spirit. They have no purpose or goal. Jane is their opposite; she's free. The most beautiful person I know."

Thus began yet another phase of Jane Wood Reno's life, a phase which produced many more classic stories. She was on the other end of the reporter-news connection now, creating instead of covering stories which were to become legend throughout Miami. Fittingly enough, it was in the year that she switched to full-time public relations work that the Miccosukee tribe of the Seminole Indians tied a head-dress on her and declared her Princess Apoongo Stahnegee, an honorary Seminole princess. It was her greatest honor.

Former *Miami News* humorist John Keasler met Jane at a party one night at the Everglades Hotel around this time. He was new in town, and she gave him one of her inimitable introductions to Miami.

"I want to show you something," she said. After taking him up to the roof, she led him past some construction work and told him to open a door. On the other side of the door, there was a fifteen-story fall.

"Jane, are you trying to kill me?" he said.

"No," she replied. "I wanted to show you the prettiest sight in Miami."

He admitted it was the prettiest sight he'd ever seen.

The two biggest accounts Jane had while working for Hank Meyer were the Miami Seaquarium and National Airlines, and she often planned promotional events involving both of them. One successful idea was "The Great Ghost Crab Race," where children matched their ghost crabs caught on Florida's beaches against their Californian competitors.

After the Miami Seaquarium received a plea from the small town of Cesenatico in Italy, Jane dreamed up another public relations coup. The town had a lonely female porpoise named Lalla living in a canal, pining away for a mate. The Seaquarium, under Jane's encouragement, offered an All-American boy porpoise, and National Airlines came through with an offer of transportation for the groom to Italy. John Keasler became escort and best man, and was aided by humorist Art Buchwald. Surrounded by a great hoopla, Palooza, the boy porpoise, flew to his bride in Cesenatico and fell snout over flipper in love with Lalla the second he hit the water.

In the early sixties, the Reno children were building their own lives away from home, and the porch became a gathering place for an eclectic mixture of people unrelated to the family. Janet was engrossed in her studies at Harvard Law School, Robert was living an idyllic life as *Miami Herald* bureau chief in Key West, Maggy was finishing college at Swarthmore and raising a baby at the same time, and Mark was in Officer Candidate School at Fort Benning.

Jane eagerly anticipated the birth of her first grandchild, Maggy's son Jimmy. When she heard the news over the phone, she whooped with delight. The operator asked her to stop shouting. Jane's response to the operator was so emphatic that her phone was cut off for an hour.

Without her beloved children around, Jane filled her life and porch with Seminole Indians (the first Seminole newspaper, the *Seminole Indian News*, was created on the Reno porch), journalists, politicians, lawyers, plain folks, and other people who subscribed to her open-armed approach to the world. Race, age, profession, intelligence—none of them mattered. This was the age of the porch parties, which involved drinking, discussion—sometimes casual and sometimes heated—singing, and enjoying the diverse company of attendees.

Jane learned from and shared with the Seminoles. The name Seminole, from the Miccosukee word "seminolay," is often translated as "run away," but a more accurate translation would actually be "wild" or "free." In this sense

Jane was essentially a Seminole woman. The communal aspects of the Seminole culture and their belief in the freedom of the human spirit were, as she noted, what the hippie movement later came to advocate. On the Reno porch, this sort of culture flourished without long hair or beads or any sort of conforming nonconformity, well before the Vietnam War even began.

Jane's love of spring-hopping in the cold, clear waters of North Florida remained a steady passion, and weekend trips to the Suwannee country became a ritual. Gathering up family and friends, she would lead a caravan upstate, navigating from one spring to the next with the help of a worm-ridden and pencil-marked Florida Geological Survey book. From the surface far, far above, they snorkeled and gazed at the wondrous, subterranean world, and collected fossilized alligator droppings millenniums old. Afternoons lazed by with cool melons and beer, and blue crabs netted in the grasses just off the Gulf. Jane traded stories with the boat-shack man and set camp near the boil that marks the origins of the Ichetucknee. Around the campfire, they told and retold stories until they could no longer stay awake.

Having had a coronary around 1960, Henry had slowed down and wasn't always able to keep up with Jane's boundless energy and sense of adventure. He had a settled routine after four decades at the *Herald*, and their different lifestyles meant that they spent less and less time together. Still, he continued to be an important part of her life, "serene, pleasant, and a source of strength to me." He retired from the *Herald* in 1965, as he approached his thirtieth anniversary of marriage to Jane, he was asked what it had been like.

"Has it been thirty years?" he said, marveling at the thought. "Thirty years with such a woman! Well, to tell the truth, I wouldn't have missed a minute, not for a million."

Only a few weeks after their thirtieth anniversary, Henry Olaf Reno, a Pulitzer Prize winner who had covered crime in Miami from the days when Capone wintered there to the reign of Meyer Lansky, died of an aneurysm at his cabin in the Everglades, out near Immokalee in the Big Cypress Swamp. He had been spending more time alone at this retreat, and he died in the solace of the great swamp that both he and Jane loved so well.

By now, Jane had many grandchildren, and she made up her mind to spend all her retirement money on showing them the beauty and variety the world had to offer. To her grandchildren she was known as Grandmud, and she would never tolerate being called Grandmom or any other conventional grandmother names. The "Grand" part wasn't important to her, and she told them, "Just call me Mud."

Jane's adventures with her family often took unusual twists. A canoe trip down the Wacissa and Aucilla rivers of north Florida in 1971 coincided with grandson George's fifth birthday. They had to use sticks for birthday candles and eat a crushed birthday cake. While fending off the spiders that invaded their canoes, they paddled along until they came to a dead end where the river went underground. It simply ended in the middle of the forest.

Unaware that the river disappeared and reappeared downstream and unable to paddle back upstream, the group was stranded. Jane, daughters Maggy and Janet, and Maggy's husband Jim and their kids contemplated what to do. They decided to send Jim and Janet off for help because they were the only ones on the trip who had shoes. The remainder of the group slept in a briar patch, using soggy towels for blankets to ward off the mosquitos. This outing was the baptism of her grandchildren into the Reno spirit of adventure.

About other adventures of this opinionated family, Jane once said, "Two or three Renos in close quarters is bad enough. Can you imagine three generations of us in one tent?"

Revisiting the fascinating places of her youth, she took daughter Maggy and grandsons Jimmy and George to Iran, Turkey, and Greece in 1973. They wandered the Parthenon, explored Turkish bazaars, drank at wine festivals, took a boat ride on the Bosforus, let guides sacrilegiously—and perhaps dangerously—smuggle them into minarets of mosques in Shiraz, and visited the grave of poet Hafiz. Climbing a mountain in Trebizon to visit the ruins of a Byzantine monastery, they encountered a mural that caused George to declare, "Look! Jonah wasn't swallowed by a whale. He was swallowed by a giant sturgeon."

In the next few years they journeyed to the Galapagos Islands during nesting time, when the albatross shows off its mating dance. They saw the Queensland coast of Australia from Brisbane up to Cairns, dived on the Great Barrier Reef and hiked through rainforests, and explored the hot springs, fjords, and glaciers of New Zealand. From the Down Under adventure Jane always recalled delightedly, "They called me 'Jine'!"

She retired from public relations work in 1974 and directed her energies toward improving the wonderful piece of property on Kendall, an oasis among the encroaching townhouse developments. Everywhere that there was not lawn, Brazilian pepper trees—also known as Florida holly—had begun to shade out the native vegetation. Day after day she started up the chainsaw, and swinging it about with her sinewy, gnarled arms, went to battle the pepper trees. Against Jane they never stood a chance. Simply cutting them down did nothing, because they grew back as quickly as she could cut them, so she used a special herbicide on their stumps to eradicate them completely.

The peacocks continued happily strutting through the yard, fanning their gorgeous feathers during mating season, and erupting in their ear-splitting cacophony each time a visitor arrived. When people called on the phone and wondered what was causing the racket in the background, she replied confidingly and with a touch of sadness, "Oh, that's Horace. He's mental, you know."

Thus all the peacocks came to be called Horace.

Jane was invariably an early riser, getting up with the sun and playing games of solitaire at the porch table, or sipping a beer and enjoying the quiet breeze before going out to work in the yard. Until the early 1980s, she kept up a steady regimen of at least one six-pack of beer and a pack of cigarettes a day. Her quick wits saved her more than once from arrests on drunk-driving charges. Once a state trooper pulled her over and asked her what was in the brown bag on the floor. Inside were a couple of six packs, but without hesitating she replied sweetly, "Why, dirty diapers, officer, would you like to see them?"

Eventually the odds caught up with her, and a major fender-bender brought an end to her drinking career. She managed to have the accident in Monroe County, outside the jurisdiction of either of her politician daughters. Janet got her out of jail, but insisted that Maggy take her to the trial so there would be no suggestion that the Dade County State Attorney was trying to influence the case. Jane not only faced charges for DUI and causing an accident, but she was also charged with resisting arrest and calling the officer "a baby-faced pipsqueak." She also gave up smoking around this time, though for years after she kept an unlighted cigarette in her hand "just as something to wave around."

There were fewer strange animals around now that Jane's children were grown, but possums and raccoons still roamed nocturnally, and a group of skunks showed up at one point and took up residence in the house. After patiently trapping each skunk, she would take it over in the middle of the night to a nearby police station and set it loose.

Though she loved her children unconditionally, Jane often expressed disapproval of her daughters' political careers. A vacation to England, Scotland, and Wales in 1978 had to be postponed because Janet was seeking re-election as State Attorney in Dade County. Jane scornfully referred to the campaign as Janet "getting bogged down in her foolery." At the same time, Maggy was seeking her second term on the County Commission up in Martin County,

175
▲

and Jane rebelled against the demands public life made on her daughters.

"Politics! The hell with politics! It eats up all their time. They're public servants all right, all the time, nights and weekends."

"Mother," Janet responded, "it was you who told me that politics now has the great frontiers, the great battles of ideas to be fought, the challenge of changing things for the better. I believed you, and I believe that's right. You helped lead me into this."

"I wish they'd both been disco dancers," was Jane's oft repeated refrain. "I really do."

The disapproval of career choice was merely another one of Jane's playful jabs at the pomposity and seriousness of the world, though, for she was proud of all her children and was never a person to have regrets. The pride with which she talked of them made her misgivings seem irrelevant. Looking back at the work Jane was doing as a journalist during the height of her Special Report feature days, daughter Maggy notes that it seems uncannily similar to the issues she deals with as a county commissioner.

The elder of her sons, Robert, has established himself as a nationally syndicated journalist in New York with *Newsday*, and has a feature somewhat akin to his mother's Special Reports. Originally an economics column, it has evolved into something called "Reno At Large."

Mark inherited his mother's love of the outdoors. His various careers as paratrooper, game warden, sailor living off the ocean in the Bahamas, carpenter, tree nurse, caretaker of a 20,000 acre ranch in north Florida, electrician, and tugboat captain in Nigeria, have kept him out of the confines of an office.

Having duly spoiled her grandchildren and covered a great deal of the world's surface, Jane relaxed and let herself be spoiled. Her eyesight started failing and her hearing got worse, and if asked how she was, she would reply, "I'm blind and I'm deaf, but otherwise I'm perfect!"

She never tired of collecting new stories. The Reno house retained its open air of welcome, and visitors came from all over the world. Years after Jane's 1975 visit to Australia, a woman named Dianne Brown called the house. She said she had finally make it to Florida and asked Jane if her invitation still stood. Jane had no idea who she was, but invited her anyway. The stranger turned out to be a waitress from a coffee shop in Cairns who had taken Jane up on an invitation to visit her should she ever make it to America.

When Jane was diagnosed with lung cancer, her family was determined to make the final years of their matriarch's life as enjoyable as possible. Jane set out to be a hero and Janet set out to spoil her. Janet, Robert, Maggy, and Maggy's son Bob took her to Costa Rica, where they stopped by to visit the rain forest laboratory where her niece Julie Denslow worked. Janet took her to California to visit her sister Winifred. With grandson Doug Reno and niece Sally Winslow, she and Janet crossed the entire length of Canada by train, and Janet also took her on a Caribbean cruise.

"She couldn't get around that well," said Janet, "but she loved exploring and she wanted to GO."

In the final eight months of her life, her children took her on a houseboat down the St. John's River, and Maggy and Janet travelled with her in a motor home to visit her brother George and his family in Maine. While she was in Miami, she kept up a weekly ritual of going out for lunch with her granddaughter Karin Hunter Reno, who remembers people looking on in horror as this gnarled old woman in a wheelchair slurped down two dozen oysters. Though Jane thrived on adventure, her family was her greatest treasure. Just before her seventy-ninth birthday, she welcomed with delight a new addition to the family, great-grand-daughter Kymberly Hunter Hurchalla, daughter of James and Gretchen Hurchalla.

On August 24, 1992, she experienced for one last time the power and fury that had made her fall in love with Florida sixty-six years earlier. Hurricane Andrew, one of the most compact and powerful storms to hit south Florida in this century, cut a swath through South Miami and Kendall on its way down across southern Dade County, with the northern edge of the eye passing only a few miles south of the Reno house. During the worst of the storm, Jane and Janet sat comfortably in one of the rooms of the house that Jane had built with her own hands. As the eerie sounds of 160 MPH gusts of wind whistled through the porch, they watched the tail end of the storm from out on the porch. The roof, which had been reshingled by family members in 1990, lost only one shingle, and the only other damage was to a few screens.

She enjoyed her peacocks, her porch, and her life right up to the end. On December 20, 1992, she went into a coma and on the following day, she died peacefully with several of her children holding her hand.

"She did it so perfectly," Janet said of her mother's death.

A *Miami Herald* editorial wrote of her the day after her death:

> There can be no finer epitaph than this: She did it all.

Her final wishes were to be cremated and to have her ashes spread over Biscayne Bay while loved ones read poetry—lines from Swinbourne and Spender, Shakespeare's *The Tempest* ("Our revels are now ended..."), and a poem of her own:

> *Dying and fire, being two mysteries,*
> *Let me adore them now while I may.*
> *Someday I shall be breathless and fireless*
> *My hands will look living, but I shall be gone;*
> *Because of that day, this day is so lustrous,*
> *Death will still be here when I am God.*